PREPARED FOR THE COMMITTEE ON SCIENCE AND PUBLIC POLICY OF THE NATIONAL ACADEMY OF SCIENCES

Peer Review in the National Science Foundation

PHASE ONE OF A STUDY

STEPHEN COLE
Professor of Sociology,
State University of New York at Stony Brook

LEONARD RUBIN
Consultant,
National Academy of Sciences

JONATHAN R. COLE
Professor of Sociology,
Columbia University

NATIONAL ACADEMY OF SCIENCES
Washington, D.C.   1978

Library of Congress Catalog Card Number: 78-55184

International Standard Book Number 0-309-02788-8

Available from

Office of Publications
National Academy of Sciences
2101 Constitution Avenue, N.W.
Washington, D.C.   20418

Printed in the United States of America

Foreword

This report by the Committee on Science and Public Policy of the National Academy of Sciences addresses a matter of central concern to scientists and to the general public: How are the judgments made that determine which specific basic research projects and investigators shall be supported with the funds allocated to such purposes by the Congress? The National Science Foundation is charged with assuring the continuing strength of national scientific endeavor. Accordingly, it is the responsibility of the Foundation to determine which areas of science should be supported and in what relative amounts. Within each area, the Foundation must identify those research projects that offer greatest opportunity either for advancing understanding or for subsequent application. The principal mechanism utilized by the Foundation to this end is the "peer review process."

It is the purpose of this report to describe and examine the operation of that process in light of the above purposes. I am grateful indeed to the Committee on Science and Public Policy for this effort, which should serve science and the nation well.

PHILIP HANDLER
President

Preface of the
Committee on
Science and Public Policy

Both the scientific community and the public at large want to be sure
that innovative creative research is supported as effectively as available funds permit. They believe that support should be provided not
only for the active leaders of the major scientific fields but for talented
young researchers early in their careers. Most would also argue that
scientists whose productivity and originality are declining should receive less support. In any event, the public has a right to know whether
its monies are wisely spent, whether the funds available are in fact
distributed to support research of the highest quality. It is entitled to
ask to what extent its support of particular programs in basic science
should in due course be linked to the contributions those programs are
expected to bring to the public welfare. It is entitled to wonder whether
scientists immersed in the excitement of their particular fields, con-
fined by their constraints, and often motivated by the internal structure
of their subjects, miss possible developments that would benefit the
public. In response, the scientist points to the developments of the past
quarter century, during which the technologies emerging from the rapid
advance of science in the United States have been most impressive.
The skeptics may, of course, reply that perhaps there has been more
support for science than needed or justified, no matter how many gains
can be cited. These questions are legitimate, and we have no doubt that
debate over them will and should continue.

This report is addressed to a limited but crucial segment of the wide
spectrum of questions about the federal support of science. It presents

Phase 1 of a study of the peer review system in the National Science Foundation (NSF). By peer review we mean the evaluation of proposals for research in the science disciplines by experts in those disciplines. Recently, there has been both public and congressional concern about the effectiveness and fairness of the peer review system at the NSF. Questions have been raised about whether scientists can be objective as they participate in the distribution within their own community of scarce funds for fundamental research. Could bias or favoritism significantly influence judgments of the quality and promise of research proposals? Could a careful study of peer review as it operates today suggest that some other system would produce more fundamental progress and understanding, greater creativity and innovation in science? The scientific community has been concerned about the public confusion between peer review and the political process by which funds are allocated to the total basic research enterprise. It has also been disturbed by some of the criticisms leveled at the peer review system. Most scientists believe that some form of peer review is the only way of assuring that available funds are being used as efficiently as possible in the development of their disciplines. Scientists see no effective method of deciding the merits of a proposal except by advice from experts in the field. Only such experts are qualified to judge the merit and potential of a proposal. At the same time, the scientific community recognizes that peer review has nothing directly to do with the total allocation of science funds or with the distribution of appropriated funds among the branches of science. It is concerned only with the distribution of funds in rather narrowly defined branches of science.

Because of these public concerns about the peer review process, the National Academy of Sciences (NAS) concluded that a study of the system was in order. The president of the Academy, Philip Handler, asked its Committee on Science and Public Policy (COSPUP) to undertake such a study. It was begun under the leadership of Melvin Calvin of the University of California, Berkeley, past chairman of the COSPUP. The research was done by Stephen Cole, professor of sociology at the State University of New York, Stony Brook; Jonathan R. Cole, professor of sociology at Columbia University; and Leonard Rubin, State University of New York, Stony Brook.

When the COSPUP began considering a study of peer review, Dr. Calvin asked the Coles whether they would be interested in conducting the research, and discussions between the Coles and the COSPUP ensued. As working scientists, the members of the COSPUP had firsthand knowledge of peer review systems, both as applicants for grants and as reviewers. The Coles had substantial experience in the aspects of the sociology of science pertinent to the study. From these discussions, plans for the study were formulated, and in February 1974, the Coles agreed to do the research. Leonard Rubin, who had just completed his doctorate at the State University of New York, Stony Brook, joined the Coles as a research associate in July 1975. He has conducted most of the qualitative interviews on which a critical part of this report is based.

To study peer review systems, it was essential to have access to information in an agency using such a system. The National Science Foundation and the National Institutes of Health (NIH) were the natural candidates; we chose the NSF. Peer review in the NIH might well be looked at in addition, because there are differences between the peer review processes of the two agencies.

The NSF's general counsel ruled that only a contractor to the NSF could have access to the necessary data. Although we could have sought, and probably received, funds from a private institution in support of this study, the NSF ruling dictated that it could only be carried out by a contract between the NSF and the Academy, with the Coles and Rubin acting as consultants to the COSPUP. To assure free access to essential information, a clause was included in the contract acceptance stating that the NAS would have a right to withdraw if the NSF refused to provide it the data needed to conduct an adequate investigation, or if the NSF in any way hindered the conduct of this investigation. It was not necessary to act upon the terms of that proviso.

A question could be raised concerning whether a study of NSF peer review systems sponsored by the NSF would be biased by reason of that funding support. In our opinion the consultants have been objective throughout the study and have approached the research problem with independence and professional curiosity. Moreover, the COSPUP itself is open to a presumption of bias, for it too is partly sponsored by the NSF. The interest of the committee was in knowing, first, how the system works; second, how well it works; and finally, how it might be made to work more effectively. Therefore, we assured our consultants in advance that they would be free to publish whatever they learned, whether favorable to peer review or not. In fact, a review article by the authors on this research has already appeared in *Scientific American,* October 1977.

What will you find in this study? First, it describes how the NSF decided which proposals were to be funded in 10 programs of their basic science research division for the fiscal year 1975. Second, it gives primary attention to the pivotal role of the program director in the decision-making process. Third, it contains a statistical analysis of the characteristics of applicants, such as age, institution, and citations to previous work. Fourth, it correlates those characteristics with the recipients of grants. In addition, it correlates peer review evaluation with the awarding of grants.

To our minds, the major findings of the study are:

1. *There is a high correlation between review ratings and grants made* (Table 23). The most important determinant of whether or not an applicant receives an NSF grant is the score given his or her proposal by reviewers. Over 90 percent of applicants receiving high scores are awarded grants, and less than 10 percent of applicants receiving relatively low scores are awarded grants. Currently the NSF seems, from this study, to be distributing money largely on the basis of reviewers' evaluations of the quality of the science contained in proposals. Thus, though program directors are not subject to exacting review and may appear to do as they please, they pay very close attention to the review ratings and act in accordance with them.

2. *In the aggregate, there appears not to be a high correlation between grants awarded and the previous scientific achievement ("track record") of the applicant.* On the average, considering all applicants, scientists who have published many papers in the last 10 years and whose papers have been frequently cited by their colleagues have slightly better chances to receive NSF grants than those who have published fewer papers that have received fewer citations. Since one of the stated criteria employed by the NSF in evaluating proposals is the ability of the scientist to conduct the research, it was surprising to us that the correlation between recent productivity and whether or not one receives a grant is as low as it turned out to be. Except for young investigators, the ability to perform research proposed can probably best be judged by consideration of the past record of the proposer; the lasting significance of the proposed research is a different matter, best judged by peer reviews. Perhaps one can explain the surprisingly low correlation between track record and grants awarded along the following lines. Scientists with an excellent track record are very likely to receive a grant. With the exception of young scientists, those with a poor record are unlikely to receive one. These extremes of the population under consideration are dominated numerically by those with track records ranging from fair to very good. Apparently, for this

considerably larger group, reviewers give much greater weight to the merits of the research proposed than to the applicant's previous scientific achievement.

3. *Reviewers residing in major institutions were **not** inclined to treat proposals from scientists at major institutions more favorably.* An analysis of 3,835 pairs of applicants and reviewers indicated that, in fact, reviewers from highly prestigious academic departments were slightly harder on proposals from scientists in highly prestigious departments than were reviewers at less prestigious institutions. And the former were relatively harder on applicants from highly prestigious departments than on those from less prestigious departments than were the latter. In this respect, peer review does not, as has been suggested, serve an "old boy" network in which eminent scientists look after their own interests.

4. *Age had no strong effect on either ratings received or the probability of receiving a grant.* Fifty-four percent of applicants who received their Ph.D. degrees before 1970 received grants; 46 percent did not. Forty-six percent of younger applicants (those receiving their Ph.D. degrees after 1970) received grants; 54 percent did not.

Phase 2 of this study is now in progress. It will evaluate the extent to which the program director affects the awarding of grants by his selection of reviewers. It will also try to determine what types of scientists and institutions make the most effective use of their research grants or contracts. Part of the study will include experiments with "blind" reviews, in which an effort is made to conceal the identity of both the principal investigator and his institution.

The findings in this study are based on the use of several statistical methods. The limitations of those methods are discussed in section 5 and in Appendix B. For the lay reader, the tabular analysis is probably the most meaningful. For example, compare Tables 22 and 23. The proportion of variance explained on ratings by funding history would appear small except possibly for economics. But the tabular analysis in Table 23 shows a definite trend, except for anthropology. Those who received NSF funds in the past 5 years clearly had a better chance of getting higher ratings.

We also want to alert the nonexpert that several linear regression methods, even when applicable, are not fine enough tools to detect the extremes in the range of cases covered in this study. Tables 26, 51, and 52 illustrate the point. Knowing the index, which combines citation and rank of department for a given proposal, does not markedly increase the predictability of whether a proposal will be highly rated. Yet there is considerable difference between the groups at the extremes. In Table 25, 80 percent of those *with a high index of 10* received high ratings, while only 34 percent *with a low index of 2* received high ratings. The proposals falling between the extremes dominate because of their larger numbers, and "on the average," the extremes are not strongly felt. The same can be said of Tables 51 and 52. There is a marked difference in the percentage receiving grants between the highest and lowest ranking. But the value of knowing, say, rank of current depart- ment in predicting the funding decisions is not very strong. Again, the group between the extremes dominates on the average.

On behalf of the members of the Committee on Science and Public Policy, I should like to thank Stephen and Jonathan Cole, Leonard Rubin, and, in addition, all those scientists both within the NSF and without who have cooperated in carrying out this study.

I. M. SINGER
Chairman
Committee on Science and Public Policy

Authors'
Acknowledgments

We would like to thank the many people who aided us in conducting this study. We owe a special debt to both Melvin Calvin, past chairman, and I. M. Singer, the current chairman of the Committee on Science and Public Policy (COSPUP) of the National Academy of Sciences, for their encouragement and for their suggestions for this research, and we relied heavily upon the exceptional administrative abilities of Robert Green, executive secretary of the Committee. Many members of the COSPUP, past and present, have been very valuable to us in their critical comments made on reports we have presented as the project progressed. Robert K. Merton and Harriet Zuckerman, our colleagues in the Columbia Program in the Sociology of Science, also provided many invaluable critiques of our research as it progressed. Judith M. Tanur has acted and continues to act as a statistical consultant. Jack Kiefer, Donald Ploch, and Burton Singer provided useful methodological advice. Otis Dudley Duncan provided a useful critique of an early draft. Thanks also to Stephen Appold and William Atwood, who did the computer work; to Gloria Lebowitz and Margaret Lardner, who did the typing and transcribing of thousands of pages of field notes and interviews that we collected in the course of conducting this research; and to James Dunne and Clifford C. Hughes, III, who aided in the data collection. Finally, Robert Hume made numerous editorial suggestions that improved the final report.

Throughout this research our liaison with the National Science Foundation was Dr. Jack T. Sanderson, then serving as director of the

Office of Program Planning and Management. We thank Dr. Sanderson for the aid he provided in the data-collection phase of the study. We also thank the many program directors, section heads, and division directors who willingly gave us their time and allowed us to ask them questions, sometimes on several different occasions.

Jonathan Cole thanks the John Simon Guggenheim Foundation for fellowship support during the academic year 1975-1976 and the fellows at the Center for Advanced Study in the Behavioral Sciences for their help during his fellowship year, 1975-1976.

We are, of course, responsible for any errors or misinterpretations of data in this report. We have currently completed only the first phase of our study of the NSF peer review system. A report on the second phase will be ready in about a year.

Contents

xiii

Introduction

In 1950 the U.S. Congress established the National Science Foundation (NSF) with the primary purpose of fostering and supporting basic research in the United States. In the 26 years since its founding, the Foundation has grown rapidly both in the amount of money it dispenses for scientific research and in the types of research that it supports. In 1952, the first complete year in which the NSF granted funds, it spent about $3.5 million. Today its budget is approximately $800 million. In 1952 the NSF had 88 full-time staff members. By 1972 the staff had grown to more than 1,000 (Groeneveld et al., 1975, p. 345).

Although originally the NSF was mandated to fund exclusively basic research, in recent years it has been asked to fund some types of applied research in addition to basic research. Thus, the RANN program (Research Applied to National Needs) was established with the aim of supporting research that would be relevant to current national problems. But, while the mission of the NSF has been broadened in recent years, its primary function remains the support of basic scientific research. Indeed, 72 percent of its fiscal year 1976 budget is allocated for the support of basic research. The NSF and the National Institutes of Health (NIH) are today the two primary sources of support for basic research in the United States.

The NSF has gone through several recent internal reorganizations.[1]

---

[1] To our knowledge these reorganizations had little or no substantive effect on the way in which peer review was conducted.

1

In part, these reorganizations have been aimed at providing a more rational organization of the growing number of scientific areas that the NSF has been funding. Figure 1 depicts the current organizational structure of the NSF. The National Science Board (NSB) is made up of 24 scientists and laymen who are responsible for setting board policy. Members of the NSB and the director of the Foundation are appointed by the President. The director is responsible for the day-to-day operation of NSF and for carrying out NSB policy.

Currently, the NSF is organized into seven directorates, each headed by an assistant director. The first three directorates—Mathematical and Physical Sciences, and Engineering; Astronomical, Atmospheric, Earth, and Ocean Sciences; Biological, Behavioral, and Social Sciences—fund basic research in the natural and social sciences. In the study reported here we limit our analysis to the decision-making process currently in operation in these three directorates. We are currently studying the decision-making process in Science Education and in RANN. In Table 1 we present the budgetary allocation to the different directorates in 1975-1977.

From its inception the NSF has always received applications for more grants than could be made. Thus some applications have been turned down. We are told by long-time NSF staff members that in years past the great majority of reasonably good proposals were funded. In recent years this situation has changed. The number of competent scientists applying for NSF funds has been increasing, in part because of an increase in the size of many scientific specialties and in part because of

TABLE 1   Budget Program Comparisons, FY 1975-1977 (Millions of Dollars)

Program	Actual FY 1975	Plan FY 1976	Budget Request FY 1977
Mathematical and Physical Sciences and Engineering	180.9	193.4	233.3
Astronomical, Atmospheric, Earth, and Ocean Sciences	184.1	219.3	245.0
Biological, Behavioral, and Social Sciences	104.2	110.4	132.3
Science Education Programs	74.0	64.8	65.0
Research Applied to National Needs	83.6	73.6	64.9
Scientific, Technological, and International Affairs	24.9	22.2	22.0
Program Development and Management	37.9	42.6	43.5
Special Foreign Currency Program	3.6	5.3	6.0
TOTAL	693.2	731.6	812.0

greater difficulty in getting funds for basic scientific research from other federal and private agencies. The Mansfield Amendment, passed in 1972, made it illegal for the Department of Defense to fund any research lacking a clear military application. After this amendment was passed, many mathematicians previously funded by the Department of Defense applied to NSF for funding.

Also, at the same time that numbers of qualified applicants have increased, the cost of doing science has gone up because of inflation. Thus, today the NSF is forced to decline the proposals of many competent scientists. How does the NSF decide which proposals should be funded and which declined? The central element of the procedure used to make these decisions is called the "peer review" system. In general, peer review consists of reviews or evaluations provided by working scientists or "peers"—the peers of the scientists applying for funds.

FORMAL STRUCTURE OF DECISION MAKING

The research directorates have similar administrative structures. The assistant director and staff are responsible for the overall operation of the directorate. The basic organizational units within the directorate are the division, the section, and the program. Each directorate is divided into a number of divisions (representing general disciplinary areas). Some divisions are further divided into sections (representing general subareas within disciplines). Each division or section contains at least one program. For example, the Directorate for Mathematical and Physical Sciences, and Engineering has five divisions: Chemistry, Physics, Mathematical and Computer Sciences, Materials Research, and Engineering. The last three divisions are divided into sections (e.g., Engineering is divided into Engineering Chemistry and Energetics, Engineering Mechanics, and Electrical Sciences and Analysis). The chemistry and physics divisions and the sections within the three other divisions are further divided into programs. (There are 45 programs within this directorate.)

Each structural unit is headed by a person responsible for its operation. The division director is responsible for the functioning of the division; the section head oversees the programs within the section; and the program director has responsibility for the program.

The division directors and the section heads are usually permanent employees of the Foundation. For the most part they are not civil servants but are required to observe many of the same regulations and

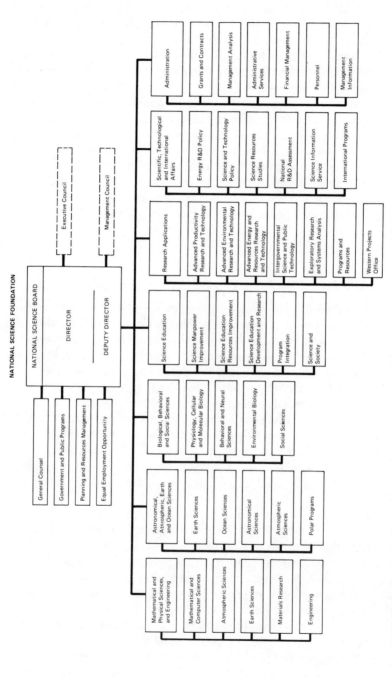

FIGURE 1   Organizational structure of the National Science Foundation in 1975 at the time of Phase 1 of the peer review study.
Source: *Organizational Directory*, NSF, 1974.

4

seniority rules as are civil servants. The program director, however, can be either a permanent employee or a "rotator." Rotators typically take leaves of absence from their prior affiliations, usually universities, for 1- or 2-year periods to serve as program directors. Currently, about 30 percent of the program directors are rotators.[2]

For the applicant, the most important functionary in the system is the program director. The program is the part of the system with which most members of the scientific community have contact. As we shall see, the program director engages in a number of activities that have a significant influence on funding decisions.

That is the formal structure of the NSF. We now turn to a description of the formal review processes within the Foundation.[3] (See Figure 2 for an illustration of this process.)

Prior to any formal review, of course, a research proposal must be developed and submitted to the Foundation. Before the proposal is submitted, however, the prospective principal investigator may hold preliminary discussions with a program director and may even submit a preliminary proposal. When completed and approved by the investigator's institution (not necessarily an academic organization, applications sometimes being received from private research organizations), the proposal is submitted to the Foundation.[4]

Virtually all proposals sent to the NSF go directly to Central Processing and from there are assigned to a division. Some applicants designate the program they are applying to, in which case the proposal is sent to the designated program office. When applicants make no such designation, Central Processing sends the proposal to a division director, who, in turn, assigns the proposal to a section. The section head then assigns the proposal to a program. Where there are no sections, of course, the proposal moves directly from the division to the program.

[2]The advantages and disadvantages of each type of program director will be discussed later in the report. Several programs also have associate and assistant program directors, including Mathematics, Chemistry and Biochemistry, Solid-State Sciences, Astronomical Sciences, Biological Sciences, and Social Sciences. Persons in these positions perform different functions. Some, in fact, do the same jobs as program directors and simply share the work of the program with the designated program director. (Associates usually have this role.) Others have as their primary function administrative support. They assist the program director in such tasks as sending out reviews and keeping track of the progress of a proposal in the system. (Assistants usually have this role.)

[3]For a more detailed, comprehensive view of this process, see National Science Foundation, "Peer Review and Proposal Evaluation, Staff Study," *NSF Peer Review Study*, 1975a.

[4]Under the law, individuals without a formal affiliation can submit proposals, but in fact they almost never do.

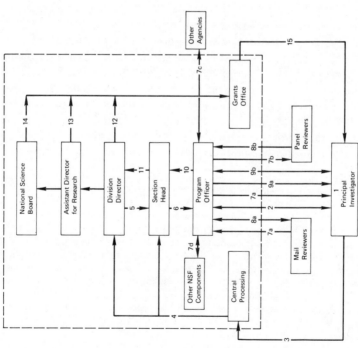

Notes

1. Principal Investigator (P.I.) conceives research plan.
2. P.I. may hold preliminary discussions with Program Director (P.D.) and/or submit preliminary proposal for evaluation.
3. Final proposal is prepared by P.I., approved by Institution and sent to NSF.
4. Central Processing assigns proposal to a Division.
5. Division Director assigns proposal to a Section.
6. Section Head assigns proposal to a Program.
7a. Program Director chooses reviewers and sends out proposal for independent mail review.
7b. Program Director may choose panel members and send them copies of proposal in preparation for panel meeting.
7c. Program Director may discuss proposal with another agency.
7d. Program Director may discuss proposal with other components of NSF.
7e. Program Director may make site visit (or site visiting team may be appointed and report back to P.D.).
8a. Independent mail reviewers evaluate proposal and return signed, written reviews.
8b. Panel members discuss proposal and indicate rating.
9a. Program Director may decline proposal but suggest some major modification that would make it more acceptable or may suggest that a new proposal may be written.
9b. Program Director may decide to recommend funding and negotiates revised budget with P.I.
10. P.D. recommends funding of revised amount.
11. Section Head reviews recommendation, approves and transmits, or rejects.
12. Division Director reviews recommendation, approves and transmits, or rejects.
13. Assistant Director for Research may review recommendation.
14. If grant is large enough, National Science Board must review.
15. Grant is made to Institution, which disburses funds to P.I.'s project.

FIGURE 2   Schematic diagram of the formal peer review process at the NSF. Source: ''Peer Review and Proposal Evaluation,'' NSF, 1975.

6

The review process begins when the proposal is received by the program director. There are two procedures for reviewing basic research proposals in the NSF: *ad hoc* mail review and a combination of panel and mail review.[5] When the *ad hoc* procedure is used, the program director, after examining the proposal, chooses a number of reviewers (about 3-10) and sends them the proposal for independent review. The selection of reviewers—how it is done and how well it works—involves critical decisions. We will discuss this selection process in greater detail in section 2. Along with the proposal, reviewers receive instructions and reviewing forms. Instructions inform them of the criteria they should use in evaluating the proposal. There are 11 stated criteria that are subdivided into four groups: criteria evaluating the principal or named investigator's demonstrated competence; criteria evaluating the content of the proposed science; criteria evaluating the relevance and utility of the proposed research; and criteria evaluating the long-term scientific potential of the research for the United States. (These criteria and the reviewing form, as they appear in the NSF publication, are reproduced in Appendix A.) The reviewing form asks the reviewer for two judgments: an overall adjectival evaluation of the proposal (rating the proposal from excellent to poor) and written comments related to the stated criteria. The program director uses the completed reviews in making his decision.

The stated criteria to be used in decision making include not only an evaluation of the quality of the scientific content of a proposal but also the past performance of the investigator and the ability of his institution to support the research. The formal inclusion of this latter criterion is important, since some people outside the Foundation have intimated that such considerations do not have a legitimate place in the allocation process.

None of the criteria sent to reviewers relates to the matter of the geographic region from which the proposal comes. Yet in the NSF Act approved by Congress and signed into law, Section 2(e) reads: ". . . in exercising the authority and discharging the functions referred to in the foregoing subsection, it shall be one of the objectives of the Foundation to strengthen research and education in the sciences, including independent research by individuals, throughout the United States and *to*

---

[5]The combination of mail and panel review is used by all programs in the Biological and Behavioral and Social Sciences Directorates and in the divisions of Earth and Ocean Sciences. It is used in Engineering for Research Initiation Grants. The remainder of programs use *ad hoc* mail review.

avoid undue concentration of such research and education."[6] (Emphasis added.) This provision as interpreted by the NSF means that given roughly equal scientific merit, an attempt should be made to see that geographic balance is duly considered in the granting process.

When the combined panel and *ad hoc* reviewing process is used, the program director, after examining the proposal, sends it out to both mail reviewers and panelists. (The size of panels, as well as the number of panelists who receive proposals to review, varies from one program to another.) The panel usually meets in Washington three times a year, and together the panel reviews, mail reviews, and panel discussion provide the basis for the program director's decision.[7]

During the review process the program director may also discuss a proposal with other federal agencies and with people in other parts of the NSF. He may also talk informally with the principal investigator in order to clarify questions about the proposal. In certain cases involving large grants the program director may make a site visit or appoint a team for this purpose.

In the end, after the reviewing has been completed, the responsibility for the decision to fund or not to fund rests with the program director. The peer reviews have an "advisory" status. The program director makes one of five decisions: (1) To fund the project or program. This decision is often followed by further negotiations between the program director and the principal investigator about the budget. These discussions produce a revised budget that the program director recommends for funding. (2) To decline due to lack of funds. (3) To decline but suggest modifications that would make the proposal more acceptable. (4) To decline but recommend that a new proposal be written and submitted. (5) To decline without recommendation.

After the decision is made, it is reviewed by the section head, if there is one, and by the division director. The division director either approves and transmits the decision to the next level or rejects it, thus requiring the program director to reconsider the action. Reconsideration is usually for insufficient documentation; the validity of the decision is not normally questioned.

Recently, a new level of review has been introduced. Each directorate now has an Action Review Board. This review board is

---

[6]As quoted in National Science Foundation, "Peer Review and Proposal Evaluation, Staff Study," p. 18.

[7]The review panel should not be mistaken for the advisory panel. The latter is a group of 8-10 scientists created on a disciplinary basis. Their function is to advise the Foundation of developments in different scientific areas and to evaluate the performance of individual programs.

chaired by the assistant director or deputy assistant director of the Foundation and is composed of both scientists and nonscientists within the NSF. It meets weekly to review all awards and selected declinations, examining whether projects are consistent with the objectives of the program; whether reviewers were appropriate; whether sufficient consideration was given to their comments; whether NSF grant policies have been followed; and whether the titles of proposed projects appear meaningful to a lay audience as well as to scientists.[8]

In most cases, review by the Action Review Board is the last stage in the review process, but some projects are reviewed by the National Science Board. Such review will take place if a large amount of money is requested ($500,000 or more in a given year or a total of $2 million or more); the commitment is for a period exceeding 5 years; or there are "important policy considerations." Few proposals require review by the NSB.

When the review process has been completed, the investigator and/or institution involved are informed of the Foundation's action. If the proposal is funded, the grant is almost invariably made to the institution with which the investigator is associated, which, in turn, dispenses funds to the principal investigator's project.[9]

Within the past year the NSF has begun to give rejected applicants more information about the content of peer reviews. In June 1975, the NSB established a policy of making available to principal investigators, on request, anonymous verbatim reviews.

COMPARISON OF NSF AND NIH PEER REVIEW

We have compared peer review as it is employed in the National Institutes of Health (NIH), the other major national agency funding basic research, with the way it is employed by the basic research directorates of the National Science Foundation. The NIH uses a review system called "dual review."[10] The NIH does not have program

---

[8]Letter from H. Guyford Stever, Director, NSF, June 30, 1976.

[9]The following figures provide some sense of the volume of cases dealt with in the review process. In fiscal year 1974 the Research Directorate received about 13,000 proposals. The success rate was approximately 50 percent. On the average, each proposal received five reviews. (SOURCE: Cumulative FY 1974—Statistics of Proposals and Actions.)

[10]For a more detailed description of the peer review process in the NIH see John G. Wirt *et al., R & D Management: Methods Used by Federal Agencies.* See also *Grants Peer Review,* Report to the Director, Phase I, NIH, Washington, D.C., December 1976. This report was released after our Phase 1 research had been completed.

directors who play a determining role in decisions on funding.[11] Rather, the NIH program is divided into approximately 50 study sections headed by executive secretaries. Each of the study sections is a panel of approximately 15 scientists. Each proposal that comes into the NIH is assigned to one of the study sections and is sent out to the members of the study section by an executive secretary. Generally, the executive secretary will ask three members of the study section with particular competence in the area of the proposal to lead the discussion of the proposal. The NIH does not make systematic use of mail reviews.

The study section meets periodically in Washington, D.C., to discuss and vote on the proposals it has received. If a majority of the study section members vote to approve a proposal, each member in secret ballot gives the proposal a priority score from 1 to 5. The executive secretary then averages the scores for each proposal and multiplies the average by 100. This becomes the proposal's total priority score. When the study section has completed its work, the executive secretary arranges all the proposals in order of priority from the top down to those not approved for funding. The NIH staff then identifies proposals that seem to have received inadequate review, have been disapproved by more than two study section members, require funding over $100,000, or are judged to be especially relevant to the Institutes' missions but have not received high priority scores (Wirt *et al.*, 1974, p. 28).

The priority scores and the proposals are then sent to the advisory councils of the concerned Institutes in the NIH. The advisory councils then decide which proposals should be funded, taking into consideration the relevance of the proposed research for the missions of the particular Institutes. But, in general, the priority scores given by the study sections determine the probability of whether or not particular proposals will be funded. Wirt *et al.* (1974, p. 29) point out that over 95 percent of proposals are never discussed at the council meetings. The following are aspects of the NIH system that differentiate it essentially from the NSF system:

1. Proposals are classified according to relevant biomedical problem areas as well as the relevant scientific problem areas.
2. All reviewing is conducted by panels.

---

[11]The degree to which the NIH executive secretaries influence the decision-making process is an empirical question. Their role is de-emphasized in formal descriptions but may turn out to be more significant.

3. The program manager in the NIH plays an essentially passive role in the decision-making process.

4. Social and medical relevance of research is more significant in the NIH decision-making process.

CRITICISMS OF PEER REVIEW

In recent years several features of the government's decision-making process on the distribution of scientific research funds generally, and the peer review particularly, have come under attack both by government officials and by members of the scientific community.

Perhaps the most far-reaching criticisms of the NSF peer review system were made during a congressional hearing held in July of 1975 by the House Subcommittee on Science, Research and Technology. This hearing was aimed specifically at the NSF peer review system. Approximately 25 witnesses, including former Representative John Conlan of Arizona and Representative Robert Bauman of Maryland, appeared before the Committee to give testimony about various aspects of peer review.

The most important criticism made of the NSF peer review system is that it results in unfair decisions. That is, for example, scientists who are most capable of advancing science are sometimes denied grants and scientists who are doing less significant work are given grants. It was claimed, particularly in testimony given by Congressman Conlan, that the peer review system is essentially an "old boy system":

I know from studying material provided to me by NSF that this is an "Old Boy System," where program managers rely on trusted friends in the academic community to review their proposals. These friends recommend their friends as reviewers. . . .

Without any effective management control procedures to insure accountability in this kind of system, it is almost inevitable that some program managers may almost unconsciously become advocates for certain scientists and their projects. . . .

It is an incestuous "buddy system" that frequently stifles new ideas and scientific breakthroughs, while carving up the multi-million dollar federal research and education pie in a monopoly game of grantsmanship. [National Science Foundation, *Peer Review*, 1976, p. 40]

It is asserted by critics that this unfair distribution of funds is a result of the extraordinary power that program directors have in deciding who should get the funds. The program director, the critics say, is the agent of an "old boys' club" that gives preferential treatment to the proposals of its members. Eminent scientists make preferential evaluations of the proposals of other eminent scientists to whom they are favorably disposed and deny funds to people who are not part of the "inner circle." The program director is able to lay the ground for this because while his decisions must be reviewed at two levels higher in the organization, in many cases this review is *pro forma*. A recent Office of Management and Budget memorandum (1975) asserted that peer review "produces an unavoidable conflict of interest situation for the scientists who serve as consultants because they determine the allocation of research funds that they also receive" (Office of Management and Budget, 1973, pp. 1-5).

Moreover, say the critics, the reviews received by the program director are only advisory and the program director is free to ignore them. Program directors, it is argued, can predetermine the outcome by selecting reviewers who, they know, will be either hard or lenient on particular proposals. Even if the program director has to make a grant he would prefer not to make, he can effectively stifle the research by reducing the size of the budget. In effect, there is no way of challenging decisions made by the program director.

In order to protect this old boy system, it is claimed, the National Science Foundation cloaks its activities in secrecy, denying congressmen and others access to verbatim reviews and to the names of reviewers of particular proposals. Thus the old boy system is allowed to go on unrestrained, and effective oversight of the NSF by Congress is prevented. It is argued further that the peer review system may stifle innovative research because eminent scientists serving as reviewers may reject ideas that differ from their own.

Other frequent criticisms of the peer review system are:

1. It takes the decision-making power out of the hands of elected officials and their appointees and puts it into the hands of people who are not accountable to the public.[12]

2. It enables the scientific community to use public funds for its own

[12]An OMB memorandum, which has not been published, was distributed to members of the COSPUP at its meeting of June 16-17, 1973. Part V of the document is a summary of criticisms of the peer review system that have appeared over the past 10 years in reports of congressional committees, in articles and letters in *Science,* etc. The document has been reproduced in "National Science Foundation Peer Review Special Oversight Hearings," Subcommittee on Science, Research and Technology, U.S. House of Representatives, July 22-24, 29-31, 1975, pp. 537-544.

purposes, that is, "pure" research, while ignoring the pressing needs of society that might benefit from "applied" research (Office of Management and Budget, 1973, pp. 1-5).

3. It discriminates against scientists working in small science departments at low-prestige universities and colleges.

4. It does not weight adequately the opinions of nonacademic scientists on the merits of proposals. Most mail reviewers and panelists are scientists from prestige universities.

5. It fails to screen out proposals of questionable scientific merit. Senator William Proxmire of Wisconsin has been giving what he calls "golden fleece of the month" awards to projects funded by federal agencies that he believes are of little, if any, merit or utility. Implicit in this criticism is the question of whether the peer review system is sufficient for identifying meritorious research proposals.

REVIEW OF LITERATURE ON PEER REVIEW

Until now there has been very little systematic investigation of how governmental agencies distribute funds for scientific research. The work that has been done can be divided into three categories: (1) general studies of peer review; (2) studies of factors affecting the granting of awards; and (3) studies of outcomes of the review process.

In the first category, perhaps the most thorough investigation of peer review was conducted by the Woolridge Committee in 1965. This study reviewed the peer review process in the NIH and found the decision-making system operating effectively. The Woolridge Committee concluded:

The opinion of the Committee, based on the extensive investigations of its consultants, is that the large majority of the intramural and extramural research supported by NIH is of high quality. We strongly approve the peer evaluation method of selecting recipients of extramural grants. [Biomedical Science and Its Administration, 1965, p. 3]

The Woolridge Report was essentially a formal description of how peer review in the NIH operates. In 1974, Wirt *et al.* described in a comprehensive report the management of research and development projects in a number of major federal agencies. The report stands as the best source on the formal structure of peer review.

Recently, Thane Gustafson reviewed the literature on peer review and found very little systematic information on how peer review works in the various governmental agencies. However, referring to several "in-house" studies and several other unsystematic studies, Gustafson reviews the criticisms of peer review by Congressmen Bauman and Conlan and concludes that the available information does not warrant any major changes in the peer review system (Gustafson, 1975).

In the second category, a few studies have been done on the effects of characteristics of principal investigators on the probability of receiving grants. Douglass and James (1973) found that between 1966 and 1972, young investigators had a good chance of receiving funds from the NIH. Despite rising declination rates, they found that the proportion of grants going to new investigators remained constant throughout the period.

A study by C. C. Laveck *et al.* (1974) showed that, in the National Institute for Child Health and Development, young people and women have just as good a chance of receiving grants as do older investigators and men. They also found, however, that the young and women received less money on the average than older male investigators.

Small (1974b), in a report to the National Science Foundation entitled, *Report on Citation Counts for National Science Foundation Grant Recipients and Non-Recipients,* found that in most of the fields he investigated, there was a significant difference between the numbers of citations to the work of grant recipients and those to the work of nonrecipients. Grant recipients were for the most part more likely to be highly cited. On the other hand, an internal study conducted by the NSF chemistry section when it was under the direction of M. Kent Wilson reported that the correlation between proposal ratings and numbers of citations to principal investigators was relatively low.

Hensler, in a 1976 report prepared for the Committee on Peer Review, National Science Board, and the Committee on Science and Technology, U.S. House of Representatives, examines the subjective perceptions of NSF peer reviewers and applicants concerning the strengths and weaknesses of the NSF peer review system. In general, these two groups perceived the peer review system as "acceptable" but having some definite weaknesses. Hensler's study is based upon data from a mail survey of 1,068 reviewers of NSF proposals and 2,684 applicants for NSF funds in late 1975 and early 1976. Among other results reported, respondents frequently called for improvements in reviewer-selection procedures (more than a third being in favor of some random selection process), although there was little agreement among them on exactly what those improvements should be. Subjective assessments of the fairness of funding decisions were not related to "academic generation, institutional affiliation or region. . . . About seventy-three percent of the applicants including both grantees and declinees would favor NSF adopting a formal appeals system" (pp. v-vi). Another set of findings suggests that a "majority of reviewers and applicants believe that the NSF peer review process favors proposals from well-known institutions, proposals by older, well established P.I.'s and proposals which are 'in the mainstream' " (p. vii). Hensler acknowledges that her data cannot be used to test the accuracy of these perceptions. The data reported in our study will be useful in testing these perceptions.

A recent article attends to the grant-allocation process at the NSF. Pfeffer *et al.* (1976) investigate the proposition that faculty members on NSF advisory panels give applicants from their institutions a preferred chance of receiving grants. They conclude that this is indeed the case in the four social science disciplines studied: economics, social psychology, sociology, and political science. How this works, however, is not well explicated. Is it a result of particularism or of other unexplained variables, such as greater knowledge of the granting system among faculty members in departments represented on panels?

Groeneveld *et al.* (1975) have studied the social characteristics of advisers to the NSF from 1950 to 1972. Their study leads them to conclude: "Given the high rate of turnover observed, our data suggest . . . that no single group clearly dominates decision-making in advisory positions."

Liebert (1976) has studied the determinants of success in getting grants by examining a subsample of 5,687 from a total of over 40,000 respondents to a 1972-1973 study of faculty members at 259 American senior colleges and universities. The data set did not include information on the size or substance of grants but only on the number received and the source. There were several findings of particular interest. A surprisingly high proportion of the subsample reported having received grants. "Among all scholars in the subsample, 34.5 percent were grant-supported PIs in 1972-73 (21.5 percent in four-year colleges; 44.4 percent in universities)" (p. 666). Liebert was particularly interested in estimating the relative weights of individual productivity and other characteristics of the applicants in predicting the number of self-reported grants. He concluded: In general, we have evidence of a broadly based system for the distribution of research grants that is more competitive with regard to individual productivity criteria than it is biased by field favoritism. There is very little evidence of situational or personal particularism in the all-faculty nationwide data analyzed here" (p. 672).

In the third category, the most systematic study to date of the outcomes of peer review was published by the Rand Corporation in

1974: *Peer Review, Citations, and Biomedical Research Policy: NIH Grants to Medical School Faculty,* by Grace Carter. This report presents data from a study of more than 750 grants made to biomedical scientists working in medical schools and presented two significant findings: first, that the priority score received by a grant on its first evaluation was correlated $r = 0.40$ with the priority score received by the same grant when it was submitted for renewal; second, that the grants that yielded the most highly cited articles were only slightly more likely to have received high-priority scores when they were originally evaluated. Carter interprets these results as being evidence that:

The later study sections, though composed for the most part of different people, verified the earlier study section's selection of the set of grants that were awarded good enough priority scores to fund. The concept of 'scientific merit' obviously contains enough objective content that different groups of people meeting several years apart will agree that one set of grants is more scientifically meritorious than another set of grants. (Carter, 1974, p. 18)

These moderate correlations, however, could be interpreted as supporting the position that it is very difficult for peer reviewers to predict the extent to which a particular proposal will yield significant research. Carter's study contains analysis only of grants affirmatively acted upon. What we are really interested in is the difference between grants made and grants not made. Are grants being given to scientists who will use the funds most profitably for scientific advance? Although it might be difficult to distinguish grants that will have significant scientific effects from those that will not, it might not be so difficult to distinguish grants that deserve funding from those that do not. Further research is needed on this important question.

Several published studies suggest that peer review is not a precise process. For example, Vivona and DoVan Quy (1973) compared priority scores given to scientific proposals submitted to both the National Institutes of Health and the American Cancer Society. They found a significant correlation between the ratings given, but that it was far from perfect. In some cases one agency gave high priority scores to proposals rated low by the other agency.

Small (1974a), in a report to the NSF entitled *The Characteristics of Frequently Cited Papers in Chemistry,* reports a finding concerning the reliability of peer review judgments. Small found no significant correlation between numbers of citations[13] eventually made to chemistry papers and the evaluations of those papers by journals at the time they

---

[13]See pages 121-122 for comment on some limitations on use of citation index.

were submitted. It has been pointed out frequently that research proposals are more difficult to evaluate than papers submitted for publication. A paper can be judged by something completed, whereas a proposal must be judged by something promised. If predictability based on finished products is weak, we would expect it to be even weaker when based on proposals.

DESCRIPTION OF THE RESEARCH

Review of the literature on peer review suggests that very little is known about how it works in governmental agencies. The research reported on here was directed toward increasing our knowledge in this area. We began by studying how the peer review system works in the parts of the NSF that fund basic research and then moved to studies of other NSF divisions. Data are now being collected for an analysis of how peer review works in the Science Education Directorate. Most of the criticisms of the peer review system within the NSF have been directed toward projects sponsored by the Science Education Directorate, in particular ISIS and MACOS.[14]

In Phase 1 of our research, reported here, our primary purpose is to determine as exactly as we can how peer review works in day-to-day operation of the Foundation. Where does the peer review system in practice diverge from the formal statement of how peer review is supposed to work? Our data are well suited for throwing light on this question and also for pointing up problems with peer review. Problems were revealed in discussions with the people administering the peer review system and by close analysis of the quantitative data. The research is not suited for definitively answering the question of whether the peer review system is an "equitable" one. Although our data allow us to speculate usefully on this question, a more definitive answer awaits the completion of Phase 2 of our research.

Our analysis has led us to believe that probably the most important person in the operation of the peer review system in the NSF is the program director. Therefore, we concentrate throughout the analysis on the tasks performed by the program director and the styles in which they are performed.

The major questions that will be addressed include:

1. What is the role of the program director in determining who gets NSF funds?

[14]ISIS is the acronym for "Individualized Science Instructional System"; MACOS stands for "Man: A Course of Study."

2. Do eminent reviewers give favorable treatment to the proposals of eminent colleagues?

3. To what extent do eminent scientists receive higher ratings on their proposals than noneminent scientists?

4. To what extent do eminent scientists have a better chance of receiving NSF grants than do noneminent scientists?

The findings presented in this report are based on data from three sources.

1. We conducted tape-recorded, in-depth interviews with 70 scientists who have been involved at all points in the peer review system. We concentrated, however, on NSF program directors. We interviewed 35 current and former program directors. We also interviewed members of NSF advisory panels, members of peer review panels, and higher-level NSF officials, including section heads, division heads, and the director and associate director of the Foundation. These interviews ranged in length approximately from 1 to 3 hours. The typewritten transcripts of these interviews constitute a file of more than 2,000 pages of descriptive material on the NSF peer review system. Qualitative interviews such as we have conducted are not suited for testing hypotheses. They are, however, most suitable as descriptive material on how an organization operates and for suggesting hypotheses requiring further research.[15] The purpose of the interviews was not to find out the opinions of specific individuals or how particular program directors or other officials do their jobs, but to find out in a broader way how the organization operates and what some of its problems are.

2. A second source consists of quantitative data collected on 1,200 applicants to the NSF in fiscal year 1975. For each of the 10 NSF programs studied we selected approximately 120 applicants, half of whom were successful and half unsuccessful. The aim of this part of the research was to determine the correlates of getting an NSF grant. We faced a major conceptual decision in selecting a sample of proposals. We could sample a small number of proposals from a large number of programs, or we could be more selective and sample a larger number of proposals from a more limited number of programs. The first alternative would allow us to generalize to all the applications received by the basic science directorates in the Foundation. However, since our preliminary qualitative analysis led us to believe that there were

---

[15]Since the interviews were conducted with the promise of confidentiality, we will not identify the sources of quotations.

significant differences in the operation of different programs, using all the programs might result in obscuring differences among them. We, therefore, took the second option, selecting 10 different programs and analyzing approximately 120 applications made to each of the programs in fiscal year 1975. A more complete discussion of factors taken into consideration in sampling is presented in Appendix B.

3. Our third source of information was the "jackets"[16] of 200 of the 1,200 applicants. For each of the 10 programs a sample of 20 jackets was selected. We examined the comments by both *ad hoc* reviewers and panel members; the summary and decision of the program director; all correspondence; the proposal; the review of the decision. Notes were taken on these files. Where decisions were ambiguous we reinterviewed program directors with the jackets in hand. We also examined the jackets of about 50 additional cases that our statistical analysis identified as unusual, for example, an extremely eminent scientist whose proposal was declined or a scientist with no past "track record" who received a grant.

This study has particular strengths and weaknesses that should be pointed out. It is, to our knowledge, the first study of its kind to have complete access to confidential files and confidential reviews for both accepted and declined applications. The files and the reviews contained in the files proved to be extremely important in analyzing the significance and meaning of the results of our quantitative analysis.

For lack of time and resources, we limited the study to only parts of the NSF and, within those parts, to only 10 specific programs. We have not yet been able to interview applicants who are dissatisfied with the way they have been treated by the NSF. More importantly, we have no independent measure of the quality of the science proposed in a proposal. In order to answer definitively many of the questions posed by critics of the NSF, we must know whether the science contained in a proposal is of high, medium, or low quality. In Phase 2 of our research we shall obtain an independent measure of quality. Without this indicator many of our results must remain tentative.

---

[16]"Jackets" refers to the NSF files on particular proposals. For each proposal, the jacket contains comments by *ad hoc* reviewers and, when panels are involved, by panel members; summary and decision of the program director; all correspondence; the proposal; and any review of the decision.

Program Director Activity Prior to Decision Making

PREPROPOSAL ACTIVITY OF PROGRAM DIRECTORS

Program directors deal with applications that are submitted to the Foundation. Clearly, the population of applicants for NSF grants is not necessarily representative of the population of American scientists. While all studies of the allocation of federal research funds to scientists have concentrated on the procedures employed by the agency in reaching decisions, it is just as important to understand the factors that determine whether or not scientists apply for funds at all. Legally, any person, and certainly any American scientist, has the right to apply to the National Science Foundation for research funds, but many do not.[1]

The number of scientists competing for NSF funds varies, of course, from field to field, depending upon several factors, one of the most important being the availability of other sources of research support. For example, in mathematics apparently very little support is available from other governmental agencies. Therefore, a relatively high proportion of mathematicians apply for funds from the NSF. If we considered all scientists currently employed in Ph.D.-granting institutions in the United States, we would find that a relatively small proportion of those scientists apply for NSF research funds. Factors that determine whether

---

[1] Useem (1976), in a questionnaire study based upon self-reports, found that 25 percent of anthropologists, 52 percent of economists, 46 percent of political scientists, and 37 percent of psychologists said that in the last 5 years they had not applied for *any* federal funds.

or not an eligible scientist applies for funds are referred to as *self-selection.*

To understand a system distributing limited resources, we must know why some choose to compete and others don't, as well as the procedure used to distinguish among competitors. If the average quality of applicants for funds is high, then deciding among the applicants is very difficult. Correlatively, if there is a great degree of variation in the quality of the science proposed and in the track records of applicants, the task of distinguishing between those who do and those who do not deserve support is somewhat easier. If self-selection mechanisms make decision making more difficult, they also reduce the costs of inefficiency within the decision-making process. If the organization is judged by the quality of the awards that it makes rather than its failure to award meritorious proposals, the average quality of applicants will in large measure determine the quality of the job the agency is doing.

We have collected limited, and thus incomplete, data on the self-selection of applicants to the NSF. These data require further analysis and study. On the basis of preliminary examination, these data clearly indicate that, on average, applicants for NSF funds have more impressive track records as scientists than either American scientists in general or scientists at Ph.D.-granting departments rated in the 1971 American Council on Education (ACE) study of graduate institutions (Roose and Andersen, 1971). In evaluating the results presented throughout this report, we should keep in mind the probability that we are dealing with applicants who are not representative of American science as a whole, but who are more representative of productive research-oriented scientists. We examine next the extent to which the activities of NSF program directors influence the types of proposals they receive.

Prior to the actual review process, program directors engage in a variety of activities that significantly affect what is ultimately funded. These activities can affect both the areas that may or may not be funded by a program and the form of the proposals that are submitted to the program.

According to the NSF, the research proposed for funding by the scientific community is more a function of that community's independent assessment of the direction that research should take than of what NSF staff deems to be significant. In this view, the Foundation is quite passive; it elicits scientific judgment and acts on the basis of that judgment by providing material support for research. According to this view, the program director does not have to play an active role in seeking particular proposals. This process of "notification" by the scientific community has been referred to as "proposal pressure." The content of the program, then, is largely determined by these outside judgments.

This view sees the program director functioning to maintain a network that will facilitate this information exchange. One program director described his role in this regard:

We do not see our role as pushing the community into whatever we perceive as important to us. We do see our role as trying to identify in the scientific community what people who are particularly capable think is important.

Other program directors expressed a similar point of view; they saw their role as a reactive one. However, some program directors described themselves as being much more active in shaping the direction of research in their programs. They did not agree that proposal pressure was always a good indicator of the directions programs should take. Some of them pointed out that scientists respond to fads and that sometimes the most faddish topics are not the most important ones.

One program director talked about his orientation in the following way:

I have, contrary to the usual practice in this division, publicized rather widely areas where I thought we were making some advances, or where we were not getting good ideas, or where we were just getting replications where we didn't need them. I have gone around suggesting that people develop proposals in certain areas and saying that if we could show development in these areas, we could probably increase budgets to sustain work in these areas.

This statement suggests that on the basis of his own judgment and the opinion of members of the relevant scientific community, the program director can and sometimes does take the initiative to stimulate certain lines of inquiry. Thus, he not only assesses the state of affairs in his field but also can try to facilitate or impede certain kinds of research.

In short, program directors adopt differing styles in stimulating research. They can be influential in determining who applies to the program. Program directors who are active in shaping the substance of their programs may, advertently or inadvertently, cause some people to decide not to apply for NSF funds. This is where self-selection and social selection (or institutional selection) merge. If it becomes widely known that a particular program director favors one type of work over others, it should not be surprising when he receives few proposals representing an out-of-favor work style. The extent to which potential applicants consider the preferences of program directors is worth further investigation.

Program directors can influence the types of proposals submitted to the NSF through contact with prospective applicants. All program directors interviewed acknowledged that they had had some contact with prospective principal investigators prior to submission of formal research proposals. This contact ranges from telephone calls to program directors to inquire whether there is interest in particular areas to submittal of draft proposals as means of preliminary exchanges of ideas between prospective principal investigators and program directors.

Attitudes toward contact with applicants prior to formal proposal submission vary among program directors. Some actively encourage such contact and, in fact, are quite specific about what they would like to see. One person said the following:

There has been an elaborate process of critiquing preproposals and in trying to send out clear signals as to what is a compatible (with the program) proposal and what is not. I think it has improved the quality of the proposals we get.

Others encourage contact but insist that program directors should not try to encourage applications in specific areas. One person said this:

Probably 50 percent of the people talk to me for either real or imagined reasons before submitting. Often people will ask questions about how the system works or are we interested in their particular thing. At times it takes me a long time to convince them that I am really interested in the best science that money can afford and that I don't have a particular shopping list.

Another talked about how his involvement in this activity was mostly with young scientists. He said:

Actually, what I'm doing is giving them a course in grantsmanship, the art of writing a proposal. A young person can have a delightful idea, but if he presents it in a crummy way, he's going to get zapped. What I want to do is make him competitive enough so that people will not be turned off by the way he presents the thing.

Other views about preproposal contact are seen in the statements by the following program directors. One said:

I don't like to do it because it does put you in some sort of a position to make some kind of judgment about it beforehand.

Another put it this way:

We avoid that [preproposal consultation] like the plague. We refuse to give them ideas about how it ought to be written. Otherwise, that would put us in a bad way if we helped write it.

The attitudes and actions differ, but the possibility of preproposal contact with the program director—officially neither proscribed nor prescribed—exists for all. These negotiations can either "cool out" applicants so that they do not even apply or "heat them up" so that they do. To what extent do prior negotiations make explicit to scientists the standards of review? What types of scientists use these informal contacts? How are they used? Is prior contact useful in reducing the number of substandard proposals submitted? Although we have no direct evidence on this, scientists who have been funded by a program for a long time probably are more likely to discuss their renewal applications with program directors prior to formal submission than are new applicants. Further work on this aspect of the process is required to provide answers to these questions.

In sum, there is considerable variation in the extent to which program directors attempt to influence the forms that their programs will take. Regardless of how much initiative the program director takes, it is important that the opportunity for such initiative is permitted by his position in the structure of the organization.

PREREVIEW EVALUATION BY PROGRAM DIRECTORS

When a proposal is sent to the program, the program director decides whether or not it has been correctly assigned to his program. He can accept the proposal or he can attempt to have it transferred to a more appropriate program. If the proposal cannot be reassigned, it remains where it was originally sent, but it is at some disadvantage, since the program director may see its topic as marginal to his field.

After the proposal has been accepted for review by a program, the process of evaluation begins. The first step in this process usually involves some initial screening of the proposal by the program director. Again, program directors vary greatly in the degree to which they get involved in the initial review process.

Some directors read every proposal and make some kind of preliminary evaluation. The following illustrates this:

I would read every one of them. I have sometimes a long page written but usually a short page written on each one before the panel meeting. I would also have a number written down in the corner which nobody else would see—it was my own evaluation of it.

But many program directors give proposals only a cursory scanning before sending them out for review. One described it in the following way:

I don't read it in detail, usually. I pick a list of reviewers and send a form letter along with it.

These differences can be attributed to a number of factors. As we have noted, program directors have different styles; they have a good deal of discretion in designing review procedures. Another factor is the volume of proposals, which affects the amount of time a program director has for initial reviews.

The presence and size of ancillary staff (assistant and associate program directors) assisting with administrative details, for example, logging reviewers used and completed reviews, may influence the extent to which the program director can become involved. Such support allows the program director to spend more time in reading and evaluating proposals.

In addition to preliminary evaluation, other kinds of assessments are made at this stage. Some program directors spoke of a sorting process, which one described as follows:

I have certain subdisciplines within . . . What I will do is take the proposals and pile them up according to their subdiscipline—the ones that I want to compare with one another, the ones that can be compared with one another by experts outside.

The program director quoted above talked about decisions made on the basis of the substance of proposals. Others talked about making initial distinctions on the basis of the characteristics of applicants. One said:

We do the screening and see if it is a very well-established scientist who is already receiving a large research program but going for additional support, is it a young investigator just getting started, is it somebody so far out of it that this proposal is not even a proposal?

This preliminary work leads to selecting both who will review and how many reviewers will be chosen. Regardless of any evaluation, all proposals do go out for review. No cases were reported in which no reviews were solicited. Since time and work pressure is great, decisions made at this point are intended to make the review process as efficient as it can be. One program director described such a decision:

We might decide that a proposal that we consider is a poor proposal (and these are very few and far between) might only be sent to three or four people for review. I think the decision is made then simply on the basis that it takes a long time to review a proposal, and we don't want to waste people's time by requiring them to review poor proposals.

Thus, this work sets the stage for perhaps the most significant aspect of the review process—the selection of scientists to review proposals.

SELECTION OF PANEL MEMBERS

Some NSF programs use review panels in addition to *ad hoc* mail reviews. Program directors play a central role in selecting panel members and in administering panel reviews. Panel members are selected by program directors after consulting with section heads or division directors, or both. According to our interviews, the program director's choice of panelists is rarely overruled by his supervisors. It is interesting to note that, at the NIH, where all proposals are reviewed by panels or "study groups," panelists are selected by the executive secretaries. Thus, while the role of the NIH executive secretary is assumed to be less influential than that of the NSF program director, they have the same discretion in selecting panel reviewers.

Our interviews with program directors and section heads identified seven considerations that affect the recruitment of panelists in varying degree. These are:

1. A balance of substantive interests on the panel. Proposals in different substantive areas require an appropriate range of expertise among panelists.
2. Broad general competence. Although their specific expertise is needed, it is also desirable to have panelists who can evaluate the broader implications of proposed research.
3. The background of the program director. He will try to select people who are knowledgeable in areas in which he is not.
4. Geographic distribution. An attempt is made to ensure that all regions of the country are represented.
5. Age. The panel should include both younger and older scientists.
6. Ability of panelists to handle a heavy reviewing load. Panel review is a demanding process.
7. Ability of panelists to work together. They must be compatible and mutually responsive.

What sources of information do program directors use in selecting panelists? In some cases the program director has no direct knowledge of people in certain areas. He then has to rely on his professional networks. As one put it:

In areas where I was not particularly familiar, I would go through two steps. One, I would talk to people within the Foundation who had expertise and knowledge and solicit names from them. Secondly, I would go to professional societies and solicit suggestions from them.

Personal experience probably remains the most important factor in selecting panelists. Many program directors talked of obtaining recommendations from present panelists about possible replacements. One described it this way:

You consult your panel alumni and your present panelists. They throw into the hopper suggestions. This could be viewed negatively as a self-perpetuating dynasty. I view it as input from people whom I respect.

It is possible to view the idiosyncratic and personalistic ways in which most program directors select panel members as being part of an "old boy system." Concluding that panelists are frequently selected through an old boy system, however, does not tell us whether the method of selection influences the decision made. Panelists selected in a particularistic way might make very equitable decisions, and panelists selected in a universalistic way might make very inequitable decisions. We shall address this question again later on in the report.

After panels have been chosen, program directors assign proposals to panelists. This varies from program to program. In some cases, panelists receive all the proposals for a particular session and are free to review as many as they want (the expectation being that they will certainly review those that fall within their areas of expertise). In other cases, panelists are assigned specific proposals to review. Not all panelists are required to write reviews.

The program director has considerable administrative responsibilities in this reviewing system. He must initiate and process two types of reviews—panel and mail. After the panelists return their ratings to the program director, he records them on a tally sheet that is presented to the panelists at a session in Washington. During the discussion of a specific proposal, the program director may present some of the *ad hoc* reviewers' comments to the panelists.

SELECTION OF MAIL REVIEWERS

As we noted, one frequent criticism of the NSF peer review system is that the program director has the opportunity to select a biased set of reviewers, which will ensure a given outcome. Former Congressman John Conlan maintained that:

It is common knowledge in the science community that NSF program managers can get whatever answer they want out of the peer review system to justify their decision to reject or fund a particular proposal. . . . Since program managers soon learn, like college students, which professor is good for an easy "A" and which can be counted on for an almost certain "C" or "D," it's no trick to rig the system. [Peer Review hearings]

There are two dimensions to Mr. Conlan's claim: First, that the system is structured to permit program directors to "fix" reviews; and second, that program directors frequently take advantage of this opportunity.

Every program director interviewed was asked to react to this claim. Most agreed that Conlan's first contention is valid. It is *possible* for program directors to select reviewers who will give particular types of reviews. One program director spoke for many:

They [program directors] certainly can manipulate reviews. Again, it's easy if you know anything at all about your reviewers. Like in sending proposals to three reviewers who rate anything I send them as excellent. The same way that I can find three cranks who rate anything as poor. In principle I could do that.

However, not surprisingly, program directors almost uniformly disagree with Conlan's second contention that they actually take advantage of the possibility. The person who was just quoted said in this regard:

The statement that it can happen is a very different statement from the statement that it does happen. I am not aware of it ever happening. I think you are more likely to find evidence of incompetence among program staff than evidence of intentional manipulation.

Other program directors also insisted on making this distinction between what could happen and what actually goes on. Some talked of hearing about such abuses, but they maintained that the extent of such activity was extremely limited.

Given the possibility of transgressions, why are "fixed reviews" so unlikely? First, many of the program directors maintained that predicting outcomes is not as easy as it might appear to be. As one person put it:

Out of the 100 or so people that I use, I can think of 1 who is somewhat predictable. But I've seen people send in three fairly tough reviews and then come back with a relatively easy one. It's very difficult to tell.

Second, the volume of reviewing done in a program can make it extremely difficult to know in advance how reviewers would respond:

We process 300 proposals a year—each one gets 5 reviews and we try not to use the same guy more than once or twice a year. It couldn't be possible to fix reviews with the large number of proposals that we have.

Third, most program directors claim they have nothing to gain by manipulating the process. One said:

I worry about power only when the person wielding the power has something to gain from it, and I can't for the life of me see what he can gain except the knowledge that he has listened to the people who are in the field and has managed to have the field going in the right direction.

Fourth, the program director is accountable to the larger scientific community, and such accountability prohibits acting in a self-interested manner. As one person put it:

How can a man who serves as a program director support abuses and continue to be a practicing, reliable, honorable member of the community? He can't do it. In a sense there is a guarantee, because if a person did send out proposals to be reviewed by "cronies" everyone would soon know about it and they wouldn't want him as a program director.

In sum, program directors believe that the possibility of manipulating reviewer selection does exist, and some program directors believe that manipulation goes on to a limited extent. Despite these mitigating statements by program directors, however, the question of manipulation of reviewer selection remains serious. At this point, we have no way of determining precisely the extent of such abuse. Although program directors claim that there is not, in fact, a significant amount of "review fixing" and are able to state reasons for its absence, they are clearly interested parties in the dispute. We cannot expect them to admit to widespread bias. Since bias in selecting reviewers is a crucial issue, we have investigated it further. In the next section we present quantitative data on how selection of particular types of reviewers may or may not affect the outcomes of the decision-making process. But even these data will allow us to go only so far. In Phase 2 of our research, we are conducting a study that will attempt to answer this question. We plan to send a set of proposals already processed by the Foundation out to a group of reviewers selected by knowledgeable scientists not connected with the NSF. We shall then compare the ratings given by these two groups. If the correlation between the two sets of ratings is high, this will constitute some evidence that any NSF bias in the selection of reviewers has little significant impact on the outcome of the decision-making process.

Putting aside the question of "review fixing," what sources do program directors use to obtain knowledgeable reviewers? Among the variety of sources are: personal knowledge of the field, professional contacts in the field, references used in the applicant's proposal, files in the NSF offices, journal articles, and proceedings of professional meetings.

I think the selection of mail reviewers is mostly from my personal knowledge of the field of _____ . I've given seminars at probably 150 universities during the course of the 15 years that I've been teaching and I know people. I read the journals and we have boxes filled with lists of reviewers that have been used in the past.

And:

I have several kinds of lists of reviewers; previously used reviewers. I have journals and proceedings of professional meetings. I could also look at the references in the proposal. I also have a list of the faculty members at all the universities.

Locating sources of potential reviewers is apparently somewhat less difficult than deciding who to ask to review a proposal. A large number of factors influence the choice of who and how many should review. Most program directors tried to get a mix of general and specific reviews on a proposal. One person put it this way:

Basically, I try to reach guys who are highly qualified in the field. However, I try to pick one of the group who is not as specialized in that area. He is familiar with it, but he can stand back and look at the field from a slightly different viewpoint.

The need for care in reviewer selection is especially great when work is being proposed in a somewhat controversial area. Many program directors talked about this type of case and the ways in which they handle reviewer selection. One said:

We try to send it to three types of people in these cases. You send it to the sympathetic ones, knowing their bias. You send it to some known negative critic to see if he can distill out the substance. And in between you have to rely on people who are more general, generally competent people who don't fall into a camp, but who can give you a more or less objective view on the proposal's strong points.

Another program director spoke of his more general approach to the problem:

You have to have a good knowledge of the subfields—who are working in them, what are their conflicts. You have to then have a calibration on the reviewer. You ask, "What are the conflicts—why this reviewer might or might not give you a good one."

Sometimes the research areas are so small that there is no way to get balance among reviewers. One program director described such a situation:

We had a difficult time for a while because we didn't have people outside that "school" who were qualified to review proposals. I think a lot of proposals were funded in that area and we weren't getting good independent critical judgments.

The kind of work that the principal investigator is doing also affects reviewer selection. A physicist program director commented:

We try to make a reasonable balance between experimental people and theoretical people in the field if there is a significant theoretical component of the proposal. If it is a very large proposal with the operation in a lab, you try to select some people who have had experience managing a lab in addition to the straight physics.

It's not very often that I will ask the average experimentalist to review a theoretical work, because normally that's not a good idea. However, a very good experimentalist, with theoretical overtone, will review a theoretical proposal. But more likely, I will take an experimental proposal and ask a theoretician to review it because a good theoretician is always looking at experimental results—that's where he starts from, that's where he leaves off.

Some program directors try to balance industrial and university people, in fields in which this mix pertains. One director said in this regard:

We try to get reviews from both industry and from the university. We want to get advice from practitioners, and depending on the subject matter, we can get very perceptive damning reviews from some of the industrial people.

Another set of considerations is possible connections between applicants and the reviewers. One program director said:

I check their bibliography to see whether he has any past connection or collaborative effort with the man or if he was his thesis adviser; so I avoid people who are colleagues.

The relative eminence of reviewer and proposer is also considered. A number of program directors spoke of this. One said:

When I get a proposal from a great man. I would use at least two other great men in reviews. The problem with using young reviewers versus established is that young reviewers are apt to give innocuous reviews in these cases. A more experienced reviewer is inclined to say what he thinks one way or another.

A further consideration in selecting reviewers is their "track record." One program director said:

There is one man I stopped using because anything I sent him he said was awful and he didn't give me any information.

Another expressed a similar view:

There is one type of reviewer that I tend to eliminate—the type that always gives a negative review and a very low rating. This man will give it a low one, no matter what it is.

Finally, how reviewers fulfill their obligation to return reviews affects their selection. One program director said:

Over the years we have built up this list of adequate reviewers on the basis of the number of times they returned it when you asked them. If you send them one or two proposals three times a year and you get back one a year, you don't send any more.

In sum, considerations relative to selection of reviewers are numerous. Every program director stated that selection of reviewers is extremely difficult and, also, that it is at the heart of the process. Directors must have considerable scientific and administrative expertise to make the kinds of decisions that will lead to the best possible reviews for proposals. It should also be pointed out that, although the program directors as a group are aware of the many factors that must be considered in selecting unbiased reviewers, errors are undoubtedly made.

Relation between Reviewer and Applicant Characteristics as an Influence on Ratings

Critics claim that the program director can predetermine the outcome of the peer review process by sending proposals to scientists whose evaluations of the proposals are predictable. This might be termed the "old boy hypothesis," which presumes that the proposals of eminent scientists who are members of the "old boy network" are sent to other eminent scientists who give the "old boys" favorable evaluations. Equally important, the proposals of noneminent scientists, who are not part of this network, are sent to scientists who will give them lower evaluations than they deserve. Although we have no evidence one way or the other that the program directors select reviewers with a certain outcome in mind, we can, by looking at the outcomes, see whether the data support the old boy hypothesis. Do eminent reviewers actually rate the proposals of eminent colleagues more favorably than other reviewers?

An immediate problem in testing the old boy hypothesis is the absence of conceptual clarity in the charge. The charge is that research money is allocated unfairly, but the attribution of this unfairness to "old boyism" is somewhat confusing. What is referred to by the label old boy network? There are at least three possibilities. It could refer to scientists with a common view of their fields who will favorably appraise work only by others with similar views. It could refer to social networks of friendship—made up of scientists who know each other, "grew up" together, attended the same schools, tend to fraternize, are of the same sex, and favor each other's research proposals. It could refer to social positions; that is, those scientists who have achieved eminence tend to favor the proposals of others who are similarly situated in the hierarchy of science even if they have no personal contact with them. Critics of the peer review system never specify clearly the forms of old boyism that undermine the peer review system. The data we have collected allow us to examine the claim that persons of similar rank, intellectual background, and repute favor each others' proposals. We do not have data to examine the other forms of old boyism connected with friendship patterns.

Analysis of the 1,200 applicants for NSF funds provides some data relevant to the old boy hypothesis. For each of the 10 programs we studied in detail, we have data on the characteristics of principal investigators and reviewers and on numerical ratings given. We have begun the analysis of these data by examining the rankings of the applicants' and reviewers' current departments. The data on the 10 programs are presented in Tables 2-11. They enable us to answer five questions:

TABLE 2   Rank of Department of Reviewers by Rank of Department of Applicants: Algebra

Rank of Department	Applicants, %	Reviewers, %
Top 15	17	43
Other ranked	42	25
Unranked and nonacademic	42	32
TOTAL	101	100

	Rank of Department of Reviewers, %			
Rank of Applicants	Top 15	Other Ranked	Unranked and Nonacademic	Total
Top 15	60	15	25	100
Other ranked	45	28	27	100
Unranked and nonacademic	34	25	40	99

	Rank of Department of Reviewers, Mean Ratings Given			
Rank of Applicants	Top 15	Other Ranked	Unranked and Nonacademic	Total
Top 15	1.98	1.31	1.69	1.81
Other ranked	1.75	2.14	2.00	1.92
Unranked and nonacademic	2.13	2.70	2.21	2.31
TOTAL	1.93	2.29	2.07	2.06

TABLE 3   Rank of Department of Reviewers by Rank of Department of Applicants: Anthropology

Rank of Department	Applicants, %	Reviewers, %
Top 10	12	37
Other ranked	27	15
Unranked and nonacademic	62	49
TOTAL	101	101

	Rank of Department of Reviewers, %			
Rank of Applicants	Top 10	Other Ranked	Unranked and Nonacademic	Total
Top 10	50	7	43	100
Other ranked	30	19	52	101
Unranked and nonacademic	37	14	49	100

	Rank of Department of Reviewers, Mean Ratings Given			
Rank of Applicants	Top 10	Other Ranked	Unranked and Nonacademic	Total
Top 10	2.68	$-^a$	2.67	2.55
Other ranked	2.38	2.55	2.75	2.61
Unranked and nonacademic	2.74	1.95	2.34	2.44
TOTAL	2.66	2.09	2.50	2.50

[a]Not enough cases.

1. What is the distribution of applicants and reviewers among different-ranked departments? Are reviewers more or less likely to be drawn from top-ranked departments than are applicants?

2. Are proposals from applicants currently employed in top-ranked departments more likely to be reviewed by reviewers from top-ranked departments than are proposals from applicants currently employed at less prestigious institutions?

3. Are applicants from top-ranked departments more likely to receive favorable ratings than are applicants from lower-ranked departments?

4. Are reviewers from top-ranked departments more or less lenient in their ratings than reviewers not from top-ranked departments?

5. Are reviewers from top-ranked departments more likely to favor proposals from top-ranked departments than are reviewers from lower-ranked departments?

In order to respond to these questions, we shall examine in detail the results for 1 of the 10 programs, algebra (see Table 2). The top of the

TABLE 4 Rank of Department of Reviewers by Rank of Department of Applicants: Biochemistry

Rank of Department	Applicants, %	Reviewers, %
Top 15	12	21
16-32	14	18
Other ranked	28	16
Unranked and nonacademic	45	45
TOTAL	99	100

	Rank of Department of Reviewers, %				
Rank of Applicants	Top 15	16-32	Other Ranked	Unranked and Nonacademic	Total
Top 15	17	17	17	49	100
16-32	13	22	15	50	100
Other ranked	22	20	16	42	100
Unranked and nonacademic	24	17	15	45	101

	Rank of Department of Reviewers, Mean Ratings Given				
Rank of Applicants	Top 15	16-32	Other Ranked	Unranked and Nonacademic	Total
Top 15	1.56	2.06	2.39	1.92	1.96
16-32	2.25	1.79	2.39	2.27	2.18
Other ranked	2.81	2.37	2.58	2.65	2.62
Unranked and nonacademic	2.79	2.91	2.66	2.79	2.79
TOTAL	2.62	2.47	2.56	2.56	2.56

table shows the distribution of both applicants and reviewers among different types of departments. In algebra less than one-fifth of the applicants are employed in the 15 top-ranked mathematics departments.[1] A substantial portion (42 percent) of the applicants are currently employed either in departments that are unranked or in nonacademic jobs. The reviewers are far more likely to be in the top-ranked departments than are the applicants. Forty-three percent of the reviewers are currently employed in the top 15 departments.

Do these data by themselves tell us anything about the equity of the review process? The fact that reviewers are drawn heavily from prestigious departments tells us nothing about it. Presumably, there is some concentration of talented algebraists in the most prestigious

[1]Throughout the analysis we have been forced to use the general disciplinary ratings available in Roose and Andersen (1971). There are no departmental ratings for specialties like algebra. We must therefore assume that high-ranking mathematics departments are in general the most desirable places for algebraists to work.

TABLE 5   Rank of Department of Reviewers by Rank of Department of
Applicants: Chemical Dynamics

Rank of Department	Applicants, %	Reviewers, %
Top 15	13	27
16-40	25	16
41-70	30	24
Unranked and nonacademic	32	33
TOTAL	100	100

Rank of Applicants	Rank of Department of Reviewers, %				
	Top 15	16-40	41-70	Unranked and Nonacademic	Total
Top 15	27	24	21	29	100
16-40	30	16	22	33	100
41-70	25	12	25	38	100
Unranked and nonacademic	30	14	26	30	100

Rank of Applicants	Rank of Department of Reviewers, Mean Ratings Given				
	Top 15	16-40	41-70	Unranked and Nonacademic	Total
Top 15	1.70	2.05	1.82	2.19	1.94
16-40	1.84	2.21	2.39	2.44	2.23
41-70	2.14	2.59	2.03	2.12	2.17
Unranked and nonacademic	2.16	2.64	2.39	2.59	2.42
TOTAL	2.01	2.41	2.22	2.34	2.24

departments. Many studies have shown that mean faculty prestige and
productivity are highly correlated with departmental prestige (Cole and
Zuckerman, 1976). Program directors seek reviews, of course, from the
best people in the field, and these people tend to be concentrated in the
top-ranked departments.

In the second part of Table 2, we report the distribution of ranks of
departments of reviewers of proposals from different-ranked departments. In algebra the program director was more likely to assign
proposals from applicants in prestigious departments to reviewers in
prestigious departments. While 60 percent of the reviewers of proposals from "top-15" applicants were in top-15 departments, only 34
percent of the reviewers of proposals from unranked and nonacademic
applicants are located in top-15 departments.[2]

[2]Assuming that old boyism is indeed at work, its influence on outcomes is in part
dependent upon the extent to which proposals of eminent applicants are dispropor-
tionately reviewed by eminent reviewers. The stronger this relationship, the greater the
potential influence of old boyism.

TABLE 6 Rank of Department of Reviewers by Rank of Department of Applicants: Ecology

Rank of Department	Applicants, %	Reviewers, %
Top 18	37	32
19-50	23	16
Unranked and nonacademic	40	52
TOTAL	100	100

	Rank of Department of Reviewers, %			
Rank of Applicants	Top 18	19-50	Unranked and Nonacademic	Total
Top 18	33	16	51	100
19-50	38	14	48	99
Unranked and nonacademic	30	17	53	100

	Rank of Department of Reviewers, Mean Ratings Given			
Rank of Applicants	Top 18	19-50	Unranked and Nonacademic	Total
Top 18	2.58	2.22	1.87	2.16
19-50	2.18	2.35	2.16	2.19
Unranked and nonacademic	2.63	3.05	2.44	2.59
TOTAL	2.50	2.59	2.18	2.34

At first glance, these data may be seen as offering some support for the old boy assumption. Such a conclusion would be erroneous. We do not yet know whether reviewers from top-15 departments are likely to favor applicants from top-15 departments.

The necessary data are presented in the bottom part of Table 2 (low rating = favorable, and high rating = unfavorable). The total column shows that applicants from high-ranked departments are indeed more likely to receive favorable ratings than applicants from lower-ranked departments (comparing the 1.81 with the 2.31). This fits our expectation, since we know that the most productive scientists tend to be concentrated in the prestigious departments. The column totals show that top-15 reviewers are in general slightly more likely to give favorable (low) ratings than are mathematicians employed at less prestigious institutions (comparing the 1.93 with the 2.29 and the 2.07).

The crucial question, however, is whether top-15 reviewers rate proposals from top-15 applicants more favorably than do reviewers from other institutions. The answer to this question for algebra is an unambiguous "no." Top-15 reviewers are tougher on proposals from

TABLE 7   Rank of Department of Reviewers by Rank of Department of Applicants: Economics

Rank of Department	Applicants, %	Reviewers, %
Top 10	26	35
Other ranked	29	25
Unranked and nonacademic	44	40
TOTAL	99	100

	Rank of Department of Reviewers, %			
Rank of Applicants	Top 10	Other Ranked	Unranked and Nonacademic	Total
Top 10	36	24	40	100
Other ranked	42	23	36	101
Unranked and nonacademic	30	28	43	101

	Rank of Department of Reviewers, Mean Ratings Given			
Rank of Applicants	Top 10	Other Ranked	Unranked and Nonacademic	Total
Top 10	1.70	1.71	2.08	1.85
Other ranked	2.54	2.64	2.82	2.67
Unranked and nonacademic	2.68	2.90	3.19	2.96
TOTAL	2.35	2.54	2.80	2.59

top-15 applicants than are other reviewers. The mean review given by reviewers in top-15 departments to proposals submitted by applicants in top-15 departments is 1.98. This is a less favorable score than the mean review given by reviewers in lower-ranked departments. The information from Table 2 is summarized in the first row of Table 12. The first statistical test performed is a comparison of the mean rating of applicants from the top group of departments with the general mean rating. As we see in algebra, this is statistically significant at the 0.025 level. The figures in this part of the table simply tell us whether applicants from top-ranked departments get on the average more favorable ratings than do applicants in other departments. They do, except in anthropology and meteorology. In the other eight programs, the difference is statistically significant at the 0.05 level or less.

The next section of Table 12 indicates whether the reviewers from top-ranked departments are more likely to be lenient or tough than are reviewers from other departments. Since the mean rating given by top-ranked reviewers in algebra is lower than the mean rating given by all reviewers and the difference is statistically significant, we can

TABLE 8   Rank of Department of Reviewers by Rank of Department of Applicants: Fluid Mechanics

Rank of Department	Applicants, %	Reviewers, %
Top 10	29	28
Other ranked	45	32
Unranked and nonacademic	26	40
TOTAL	100	100

	Rank of Department of Reviewers, %			
Rank of Applicants	Top 10	Other Ranked	Unranked and Nonacademic	Total
Top 10	27	31	42	100
Other ranked	26	38	36	100
Unranked and nonacademic	35	23	42	100

	Rank of Department of Reviewers, Mean Ratings Given			
Rank of Applicants	Top 10	Other Ranked	Unranked and Nonacademic	Total
Top 10	2.62	2.47	1.54	2.12
Other ranked	2.55	3.35	2.70	2.90
Unranked and nonacademic	3.50	3.57	2.76	3.19
TOTAL	2.86	3.14	2.37	2.75

conclude that, in algebra, top-ranked reviewers are more lenient, in general, than reviewers from other departments. This is the case in only 4 of the 10 programs: algebra, chemical dynamics, economics, and solid-state physics. In the other six programs, top-ranked reviewers were in general less lenient than were other reviewers.

The last part of the table shows whether there was any significant interaction effect. That is, are top-ranked reviewers more likely to give high scores to applicants from top-ranked departments than would be expected on the basis of the general tendency of top-ranked reviewers to give low scores and the general tendency of top-ranked applicants to get low scores? Given these two distributions, the expected mean rating of top-15 applicants in algebra would be 1.68, and the observed mean rating was 1.98. Thus, there is no evidence that old boyism is at work in this program. In fact, the data show that, if anything, top-ranked people are tougher on their colleagues at top-ranked institutions than would be expected.

The last column of Table 12 shows that only in biochemistry was there any statistically significant interaction. That is, only in

TABLE 9   Rank of Department of Reviewers by Rank of Department of Applicants: Geophysics[a]

Rank of Department	Applicants, %	Reviewers, %
Top 10	36	32
Other ranked	36	31
Unranked and nonacademic	28	37
TOTAL	100	100

	Rank of Department of Reviewers, %			
Rank of Applicants	Top 10	Other Ranked	Unranked and Nonacademic	Total
Top 10	31	36	34	101
Other ranked	37	27	37	101
Unranked and nonacademic	26	31	42	99

	Rank of Department of Reviewers, Mean Ratings Given			
Rank of Applicants	Top 10	Other Ranked	Unranked and Nonacademic	Total
Top 10	2.37	2.17	2.25	2.26
Other ranked	2.23	2.69	2.05	2.29
Unranked and nonacademic	3.29	2.57	2.61	2.75
TOTAL	2.49	2.44	2.29	2.40

[a]For this table the rank of department of geophysicists is based upon the 1971 ACE ratings of geology departments.

biochemistry are reviewers from top-ranked departments more likely to give favorable ratings to applicants from top-ranked departments than would be expected by chance. This could indicate some degree of bias or that in this field it is possible that reviewers in top-ranked departments are more discriminating and are more able to assess high-quality proposals. In seven of the programs, the relationship had effects opposite to those expected; that is, top-ranked reviewers gave lower scores to proposals from top-ranked applicants than would be expected by chance. In the two other programs, anthropology and meteorology, the differences were not statistically significant. On the basis of these data, there is very little evidence that reviewers were biased in evaluating the proposals of their colleagues.

We also considered the effect of the geographic location of reviewers on how they evaluated proposals from applicants in different geographic locations. The results are presented in Table 13. The first column presents the mean rating given where the geographic location

TABLE 10 Rank of Department of Reviewers by Rank of Department of Applicants: Meteorology[a]

Rank of Department	Applicants, %	Reviewers, %
Top 17	25	15
Other ranked	33	39
Unranked and nonacademic	42	46
TOTAL	100	100

	Rank of Department of Reviewers, %			
Rank of Applicants	Top 17	Other Ranked	Unranked and Nonacademic	Total
Top 17	19	33	47	99
Other ranked	15	37	49	101
Unranked and nonacademic	14	43	43	100

	Rank of Department of Reviewers, Mean Ratings Given			
Rank of Applicants	Top 17	Other Ranked	Unranked and Nonacademic	Total
Top 17	2.79	2.98	2.94	2.45
Other ranked	2.42	2.57	2.37	2.92
Unranked and nonacademic	3.34	2.92	2.97	3.00
TOTAL	2.90	2.82	2.74	2.80

[a]Ranks based upon judgment of program director.

of the applicant and reviewer are the same. The second column shows the mean rating given when the geographic location of the applicant and reviewer are not the same. If the number in column 1 is higher than the number in column 2, there is no evidence that reviewers are, in general, more likely to favor people from the same part of the country. For 7 of the 10 fields, the relationship produces effects opposite to those expected; that is, reviewers are more harsh on proposals from people in their own areas than they are on proposals from people in other areas. In the three other areas, although the relationship is as expected, it is statistically nonsignificant.

We then tested four separate hypotheses related to whether reviewers were likely to favor applicants from their own areas. For example, the mean ratings given to applicants from the northeast by reviewers from the northeast (column 4) can be compared with the mean ratings given to applicants from the northeast by reviewers from other sections of the country (column 5). Once again, the number in column 4 would have to be lower than the number in column 5 to demonstrate regional

TABLE 11   Rank of Department of Reviewers by Rank of Department of Applicants: Solid-State Physics

Rank of Department	Applicants, %	Reviewers, %
Top 10	15	19
11-20	18	9
21-60	25	32
Unranked and nonacademic	42	40
TOTAL	100	100

	Rank of Department of Reviewers, %				
Rank of Applicants	Top 10	11-20	21-60	Unranked and Nonacademic	Total
Top 10	17	12	29	42	100
11-20	31	7	23	39	100
21-60	20	10	35	35	100
Unranked and nonacademic	14	8	35	44	101

	Rank of Department of Reviewers, Mean Ratings Given				
Rank of Applicants	Top 10	11-20	21-60	Unranked and Nonacademic	Total
Top 10	2.05	2.56	1.98	1.80	1.98
11-20	1.79	1.83	1.86	1.87	1.84
21-60	2.12	2.21	2.28	2.01	2.15
Unranked and nonacademic	2.14	2.35	2.53	2.51	2.45
TOTAL	2.02	2.28	2.30	2.17	2.20

bias in reviewing. We do find a statistically significant relationship in 2 of the 10 programs, fluid mechanics and meteorology. In these two programs, reviewers from the northeast are more lenient on proposals from applicants from the northeast than are reviewers from other sections of the country.

Proposals from southerners show no evidence of any regional bias in any of the 10 programs. They are given the same evaluations by southerners as by reviewers from other sections of the country. In all, we made 50 such geographic comparisons. In only six cases did we find statistically significant differences. There is very little evidence that reviewers in certain geographic locations rate the proposals of applicants in those locations more favorably than do reviewers from other sections of the country.

For one field, biochemistry, we collected data on the citations of the reviewers.[3] We found no correlation between numbers of citations of

[3]See Appendix B for a description of how citation data were collected.

TABLE 12 Rank of Department of Reviewers by Rank of Department of Applicants: Analyses of Variance

Program	Mean Rating	Mean Rating Given to "Top Group"	Statistical Significance	Mean Rating Given by "Top Group"	Statistical Significance	Expected Mean Rating of "Top Group" by "Top Group"	Mean Rating of "Top Group" by "Top Group"	Statistical Significance
Algebra	2.06	1.81	$t = 1.96$ $p = 0.025$	1.93	$t = 1.99$ $p = 0.025$	1.68	1.98	—
Anthropology	2.50	2.55	—	2.66	—	2.71	2.68	NS
Biochemistry	2.56	1.96	$t = 4.09$ $p < 0.005$	2.62	—	2.02	1.56	$t = 2.6$ $p < 0.01$
Chemical Dynamics	2.24	1.94	$t = 2.05$ $p < 0.025$	2.01	$t = 2.38$ $p < 0.01$	1.71	1.70	—
Ecology	2.34	2.16	$t = 2.22$ $p < 0.025$	2.50	—	2.32	2.58	—
Economics	2.59	1.87	$t = 5.80$ $p < 0.005$	2.37	$t = 2.17$ $p < 0.025$	1.65	1.76	—
Fluid Mechanics	2.75	2.12	$t = 6.09$ $p < 0.005$	2.86	—	2.23	2.62	—
Geophysics	2.40	2.26	$t = 1.87$ $p < 0.05$	2.49	—	2.35	2.37	—
Meteorology	2.80	2.92	—	2.90	—	3.02	2.79	NS
Solid-State Physics	2.20	1.98	$t = 2.30$ $p < 0.025$	2.02	$t = 2.22$ $p < 0.025$	1.80	2.05	—

44

TABLE 13 Geographic Location of Reviewers by Geographic Location of Applicants: Analyses of Variance

Program	Mean Rating Where Geographic Location Is: Same for Applicant and Reviewer	Different for Applicant and Reviewer	Statistical Significance	Northeast Applicant, Northeast Reviewer	Northeast Applicant, Other Reviewer	Statistical Significance	Southern Applicant, Southern Reviewer	Southern Applicant, Other Reviewer	Statistical Significance	Midwest Applicant, Midwest Reviewer	Midwest Applicant, Other Reviewer	Statistical Significance	Western Applicant, Western Reviewer	Western Applicant, Other Reviewer	Statistical Significance
Algebra	2.14	1.95	–	1.91	1.97	NS	1.88	2.51	NS	1.79	2.01	NS	1.97	2.23	NS
Anthropology	2.61	2.30	–	1.85	2.05	NS	3.00	2.89	–	2.69	2.54	–	2.57	2.79	NS
Biochemistry	2.57	2.44	–	2.60	2.86	NS	2.38	2.74	NS	2.36	2.46	NS	2.42	2.43	NS
Chemical Dynamics	2.26	2.14	–	2.15	2.15	–	2.69	2.15	–	2.15	2.41	NS	2.00	2.25	NS
Ecology	2.32	2.40	NS	1.58	2.00	NS	2.60	2.83	NS	2.73	2.13	–	2.09	2.38	$t = -1$ $p = 0.0$
Economics	2.60	2.53	–	2.52	2.35	–	No cases	2.88	–	1.70	2.69	$t = -2.22$ $p < 0.02$	3.12	2.65	–
Fluid Mechanics	2.81	2.56	–	2.71	3.30	$t = -2.28$ $p < 0.02$	3.25	3.28	NS	2.33	2.39	NS	1.82	2.53	$t = -2$ $p < 0.0$
Geophysics	2.40	2.40	–	2.44	2.30	–	3.57	2.71	–	1.67	2.77	$t = -2.99$ $p = 0.04$	2.40	2.20	–
Meteorology	2.78	2.83	NS	2.49	3.08	$t = -2.76$ $p < 0.005$	3.50	2.88	–	2.70	2.73	NS	2.92	2.53	–
Solid-State Physics	2.19	2.21	NS	1.99	2.17	NS	2.60	2.41	NS	2.10	2.18	NS	2.43	2.00	NS

reviewers and numbers of citations of applicants. The program director was not more likely to assign the proposals of eminent biochemists for review by other eminent biochemists, at least as eminence is measured by citations. We also found no evidence that reviewers with many citations were more likely to be lenient than were reviewers with fewer citations. As expected, however, applicants with relatively large numbers of citations to their recent work, in general, received significantly more favorable reviews than applicants with relatively few citations. Finally, and most importantly, the interaction effect is statistically insignificant. Thus, there is no evidence that highly cited reviewers are excessively favorable to the proposals of highly cited applicants.

In conclusion, we find little evidence that the characteristics of reviewers interact with the characteristics of applicants so as to influence substantively the outcome of decisions. Different types of reviewers seem to evaluate proposals of different types of applicants in much the same way. There is very little evidence for reviewer bias or for support of an old boy hypothesis. We must collect additional data to test the other forms of that hypothesis.

Influence of Characteristics of Applicants on Reviewer Ratings

We have demonstrated that the ratings received by applicants are not significantly influenced by the characteristics of the scientists doing the rating—the peer reviewers. We now examine another question. To what extent are the ratings given by peer reviewers correlated with the characteristics of principal investigators, or applicants? Four essential criteria are supposed to be applied in the evaluation of applications:

1. The quality of science described in the proposal.
2. The competence of the principal investigator to conduct the research as demonstrated by past scientific performance.
3. Available facilities.
4. Geographic and institutional distribution, all other things being equal.

We can use the data on the reviews received by the 1,200 applicants we have studied to see the extent to which favorable ratings are more likely to be received by scientists in the most prestigious institutions and by scientists who have been funded by the NSF in the past.

The quantitative analysis reported in this section has two different purposes. The first is to discover the extent to which the characteristics of NSF applicants, including measures of their past scientific research performance, can be used to predict the ratings their proposals receive from peer reviewers. The second is to discover the extent to which different types of applicants with distinctly different characteristics are

47

more or less likely to receive relatively high ratings from peer reviewers.

In order to demonstrate the difference between the two questions, consider a concrete example. The first question, relating to prediction, asks: Considering the entire sample of applicants, how well do the numbers of citations to applicants' work predict the ratings of their proposals? The second question, involving comparison of vastly different types of scientists, asks: Are the applicants whose work has received citations in the top 5 percent of the distribution of citations more apt to receive excellent or very good ratings than scientists whose work has received citations in the bottom 10 percent?

In order to answer these two questions, we have employed several analytic techniques. We have analyzed the same data using scattergrams, contingency tables, and linear regression methods. All three methods of analysis are useful in answering the first question.[1] We shall show below that each method yields the same substantive conclusions. In answering the second question we depend upon tabular analysis of contingency tables.

To discover the extent to which the characteristics of applicants are taken into account by reviewers, we have used as our unit of analysis individual pairs of applicants and reviewers. Thus, for each applicant we have two to eight different pairs. For each of the 10 programs we have approximately 300-500 cases. This enables us to see how characteristics of particular types of applicants are correlated with the ratings given their proposals by reviewers. All 10 programs we studied employed the same rating scale in which "excellent" was equivalent to one, "very good" equivalent to two, "good" equivalent to three, "fair" equivalent to four, and "poor" equivalent to five. Some programs allowed reviewers to give a score between two numbers. The distribution of ratings for each of the 10 programs is presented in Table 14.

Obviously, we do not have any measure of a crucial variable—the quality of the research proposal. We do, however, have measures of the past track records of research performance of principal investigators and data on their institution and geographic locations. It is reasonable to presume that at least part of the variance in reviewer

---

[1]We must point out, however, that linear regression analysis assumes that the dependent variable is a normal distribution function evaluated as a linear function of the independent variables. We do not have enough data to test whether these assumptions are valid throughout the study. In fact, some of the tables show that the linearity assumption does not hold. In these cases the tables give more information than probit. (See Tables 23 and 54 and the discussion of them in the text.)

TABLE 14 Frequency Distribution of Ratings for Each Program

Value	Algebra Frequency	Algebra Percent[a]	Anthropology Frequency	Anthropology Percent[a]	Biochemistry Frequency	Biochemistry Percent[a]	Chemical Dynamics Frequency	Chemical Dynamics Percent[a]	Ecology Frequency	Ecology Percent[a]
1.0	78	25	74	33	82	19	84	21	106	26
1.5	20	6	5	2	12	3	26	7	22	6
2.0	122	39	40	18	115	27	139	36	117	29
2.5	19	6	9	4	19	4	23	6	16	4
3.0	58	18	37	16	93	22	71	18	63	16
3.5	2	1	2	1	7	1	15	4	4	1
4.0	10	3	33	14	69	16	22	6	41	10
4.5	1	0.3	1	0.4	3	1			3	1
5.0	5	2	25	11	23	5	12	3	30	8
Total	315	99	227	100	423	100	392	101	402	101
$\bar{X}$	2.05		2.48		2.55		2.23		2.34	
S^2	0.74		1.90		1.32		0.96		1.49	

Value	Economics Frequency	Economics Percent[a]	Fluid Mechanics Frequency	Fluid Mechanics Percent[a]	Geophysics Frequency	Geophysics Percent[a]	Meteorology Frequency	Meteorology Percent[a]	Solid-State Physics Frequency	Solid-State Physics Percent[a]
1.0	79	25	64	19	103	21	74	13	86	17
1.5	9	3	3	1	10	2	13	2	27	5
2.0	78	24	91	27	180	37	141	25	213	43
2.5	10	3	3	2	11	2	28	5	40	8
3.0	61	19	70	20	98	20	144	26	92	18
3.5	2	1	3	1	11	2	19	3	5	1
4.0	46	14	63	19	50	10	89	16	29	6
4.5	11	3			28	7				
5.0	28	9	38	11			54	10	6	1
Total	324	100	335	100	491	101	562	100	498	99
$\bar{X}$	2.58		2.75		2.40		2.79		2.20	
S^2	1.69		1.66		1.23		1.35		0.72	

[a]Because of rounding, percents may not equal 100.

49

ratings that is not explained by reference to the three factors we can measure must be related to the quality of the science proposed, or to lack of agreement among the reviewers.[2]

"TRACK RECORD" AND PEER REVIEW RATINGS

The first question we address is the extent to which scientists who have performed well in the past are more likely to get favorable reviews than are scientists who have not. It should be pointed out that some of the scientists who, in our data, appear to have poor track records are young scientists who have not had the opportunity to demonstrate their competence.

We had three indicators of scientists' past performances. Two of these are based upon citation counts, and one upon number of published papers. We have the total number of citations to the work published by scientists in the last 10 years.[3] Citations are being used as a rough indicator of the influence or quality of a scientist's published work. The second citation indicator includes all 1974 citations to the work of scientists published before 1965.[4] This is a rough measure of the reputations of scientists based upon work published more than 10 years ago.

We also examined the numbers of papers that scientists had pub-

---

[2]For descriptive purposes we present in Table 15 the means and standard deviations for the variables we have used for each of the 10 programs.

[3]Although the *Science Citation Index* lists only citations of the work of scientists on which they were sole authors or first authors, we looked up all references to coauthored papers published by scientists on which they were not sole or first authors and added those to our totals for those scientists. (We were unable to do this for anthropology and economics.) After collecting data on the citations to all work published in the last 10 years, we used a log transformation, because the distribution of citations is highly skewed. Most scientists have relatively few citations and a small number of scientists have very large numbers of citations. By using log transformations, we avoid any effects due to a few extreme cases.

[4]For this measure we do not have citations to coauthored papers on which scientists were not first authors. However, our data for papers published in the last 10 years, 1965 through 1974, showed that the total number of citations to first-authored and sole-authored papers and the total number of citations, including papers on which the authors were not first authors, were very highly correlated. In all eight fields for which we have data, the correlation was over 0.85. (Algebra, $r = 0.99$; biochemistry, $r = 0.86$; chemical dynamics, $r = 0.91$; ecology, $r = 0.97$; fluid mechanics, $r = 0.92$; geophysics, $r = 0.96$; meteorology, $r = 0.88$; solid-state physics, $r = 0.89$.) Therefore, the data on citations to work published prior to 1965 should adequately reflect the significance of older work. Citations to older work have also been treated with log transformations.

TABLE 15 Means and Standard Deviations for All Independent Variables

Independent Variables	Algebra		Anthropology		Biochemistry		Chemical Dynamics		Ecology		Economics		Fluid Mechanics		Geophysics		Meteorology		Solid-State Physics	
	M	SD	M	SD	M	SD	M	SD	M	SD	M	SD	M	SD	M	SD	M	SD	M	SD
Citations in 1974 to work published 1965–1974 (log)	0.36	0.47	0.40	0.47	1.49	0.57	1.53	0.54	0.81	0.63	0.60	0.59	0.61	0.57	1.03	0.67	0.78	0.57	1.28	0.64
Citations in 1974 to work published before 1965 (log)	0.12	0.31	0.10	0.29	0.54	0.64	0.50	0.70	0.20	0.42	0.16	0.40	0.21	0.38	0.26	0.46	0.19	0.40	0.47	0.59
Number of papers published 1965–1974 (log)	0.80	0.45	0.97	0.69	1.30	0.42	1.35	0.41	0.87	0.50	1.05	0.76	0.83	0.56	1.08	0.52	1.0	0.46	1.28	0.42
Rank of current department	3.71	1.32	3.69	1.64	4.65	1.43	4.09	1.66	3.31	1.66	3.21	1.75	3.11	1.59	2.94	1.21	2.98	1.41	3.12	1.75
Rank of Ph.D. department	1.77	0.73	1.75	0.57	2.14	0.80	1.83	0.77	1.89	0.90	1.76	0.78	2.03	0.77	2.24	1.02	2.49	1.00	1.85	0.83
Ph.D.-granting institution/other	0.83	0.37	0.68	0.47	0.71	0.45	0.90	0.30	0.68	0.47	0.71	0.45	0.90	0.29	0.83	0.38	0.59	0.49	0.86	0.34
Professional age	1.27	0.44	1.41	0.48	1.16	0.37	1.17	0.38	1.30	0.45	1.33	0.45	1.26	0.43	1.25	0.43	1.19	0.38	1.13	0.33
Academic rank	5.08	0.86	4.89	1.09	4.78	1.43	5.12	1.05	4.84	1.31	5.11	1.15	4.75	1.38	4.74	1.52	4.91	1.32	5.14	1.03
Past NSF funding history	1.53	1.91	0.63	1.28	1.67	1.78	1.31	1.65	1.33	1.70	0.85	1.49	0.91	1.30	2.21	2.05	1.53	1.68	1.25	1.63
Mean rating	2.09	0.69	2.52	1.04	2.62	0.87	2.27	0.77	2.34	0.84	2.58	1.15	2.79	0.98	2.42	0.78	2.84	0.83	2.19	0.62
Rating of panel	–		2.54	0.86	2.23	0.58	–		2.24	0.60	3.43	1.03	–		–		–		–	

51

lished in the last 10 years. These data were collected from the source index of the *Science Citation Index* (SCI). Since social science journals are not included in the SCI, and since the *Social Science Citation Index* began in 1972, we collected data on publications for social scientists from vitaes included in proposal jackets. For social scientists we constructed a productivity index.[5] These three measures are direct indicators of the amounts of scientific work produced by scientists in the past and the "quality" of that work as judged by the scientists' peers. There is now a large body of literature that demonstrates that citations are highly correlated with other measures of the quality of scientific work.[6] Although these three measures are not themselves direct indicators of locations of scientists in the stratification system of their disciplines, they may be used as indirect indicators. We have found (Cole and Cole, 1973) that scientific output as measured by both the number of publications and the citations to those publications is strongly correlated with the visibility of scientists, that is, the extent to which they are known and the evaluations of their work by other scientists, and the receipt of prestigious positions and of prestigious awards like the Nobel Prize and membership in the National Academy of Sciences.

We would expect that scientists who have produced the most work in the past and whose work has been the most frequently cited would be the most eminent scientists in their fields. We would also expect that those scientists should get higher ratings than scientists who have produced fewer papers and have been less frequently cited. They should get higher ratings for two reasons. First, one of the stated criteria of the National Science Foundation is the competence of principal investigators. Presumably scientists who have done the most impressive work in the past should be deemed most competent to do the research proposed in their applications and, therefore, should receive higher ratings. Second, on the average, one would expect that scientists who have done the best work in the past will write proposals for better work today.

Let us turn to data bearing on our first question, concerning the predictability of ratings, given knowledge of individual characteristics of applicants. Consider first the relationship between the number of citations to the recent work of the applicant and the ratings received.

[5]For a description of this index see Appendix B. We have also used log transformations on the number of papers published, since this variable is also highly skewed.

[6]For a complete bibliography of studies using citations see any one of the annual guides published by the Institute for Scientific Information to accompany the *Science Citation Index*.

TABLE 16 Proportion of Variance
Explained (R^2) on Rating by Citations
to Recent Work: 10 Programs[a]

Algebra	0.06
Anthropology	0.00
Biochemistry	0.16
Chemical Dynamics	0.14
Ecology	0.01
Economics	0.08
Fluid Mechanics	0.03
Geophysics	0.07
Meteorology	0.08
Solid-State Physics	0.08

[a]Log of citations made in 1974 to work
published between 1965 and 1974.

We have used simple ordinary least-squared regression analysis here. The cell entries of Table 16 present the squared zero-order correlation coefficient, which is simply the proportion of variance on the dependent variable, ratings, explained by the independent variable, citations to recent work.[7]

The higher the numbers the more variance on the ratings can be explained by citations to recent work. In all fields except anthropology, citations to recent work explain some variance on the ratings received. The most interesting fact about these data, however, is that citations to past work explain so little variance in the ratings. Even in biochemistry and chemical dynamics, in which citations explain the most variance in ratings received, they explain less than a fifth of the variance; in most fields, they explain considerably less. This means that scientists who have demonstrated their competence by publishing frequently cited papers are more likely to receive favorable ratings but that this effect is weak. In fact, the great bulk of the variance in the ratings cannot be explained by citations to recent work.

We examined not only the 10 fields separately, but also all 10 programs combined. Since the mean and standard deviations on the relevant variables differ significantly from program to program, it is necessary first to standardize separately all the data within each field before combining data on applicants from different programs. For

[7]In view of the shortcomings mentioned earlier regarding the linear model, it does not seem worthwhile to list the numerical values of the regression coefficient. Throughout this section we present only the proportion of variance explained, as at least a qualitatively meaningful indicator of the strength of the relationship studied.

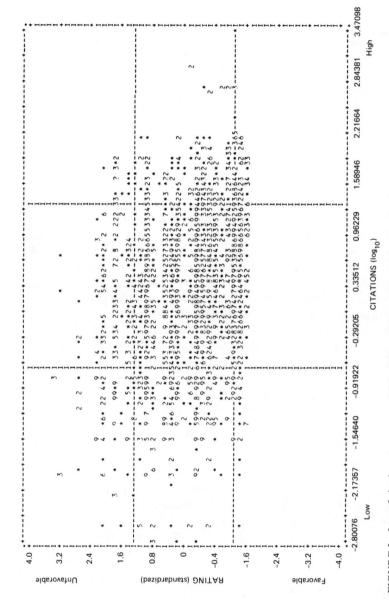

FIGURE 3 Log of citations to papers published from 1965 to 1974 and standardized peer review ratings: all 10 fields. (Note: An asterisk in the scattergram represents one case; numbers 2-8 represent that number of cases; a 9 represents nine or more cases at that point on the scattergram.)

example, we will express the number of citations received by a biochemist not in terms of an absolute number but rather in terms of the number of standard deviations above or below the mean for biochemists. Thus, a biochemist who is one standard deviation above the mean for biochemistry in citations would be treated as equivalent to an anthropologist who is one standard deviation above the mean for anthropology, despite the fact that the biochemist would have many more citations than the anthropologist. We are converting absolute scores on the variables into scores relative to other individuals in the same program. These relative or standardized scores are comparable across programs.

After standardizing the data separately within each field we were able to treat all pairs of reviewers and applicants as one sample. When we use the standardized data for all 10 fields combined, we find that citations made in 1974 to work published between 1965 and 1974 explain 6 percent of the variance in ratings.

In order to explicate still further the meaning of the results we have obtained from the regression analysis we present several scattergrams displaying the relationship between the selected variables and ratings. We begin by looking at the relationship between citations to recent work and ratings for the entire sample combined. (See Figure 3.)[8]

The cloud of points in Figure 3 indicates that there is not a strong relationship between the two variables being plotted. If citations were a good predictor of the ratings received by applicants on their proposals, we should expect that those applicants who had high citation scores, that is, were located at the far right of the scattergram, would be heavily clustered in the lower part of the scattergram, indicating that they had received "low" numerical but "high" adjectival ratings. (The reader must always invert these scores in his mind, since the NSF codes are "excellent" as a 1 and a "poor" as a 5. Between these are 2, "very good," 3, "good," and 4, "fair.") We would also expect to find those scientists who had received few or no citations, those appearing in the far left of the scattergram, clustered in the top half of the scattergram, indicating that they had received relatively low ratings on the proposals. This is clearly not the case. A substantial portion of the ratings of scientists with relatively large numbers of citations are relatively high (read low). Scientists with relatively few citations to their recent work

[8]An asterisk in Figure 3 indicates that one reviewer and applicant pair was located at this particular point in the scatterplot. Numbers 2-8 indicate the number of different pairs at those locations. The computer program used to generate these scattergrams did not have the capability of indicating a larger number than 9 at any particular location. Therefore, a number 9 indicates that 9 or more pairs were at this location in the scattergram.

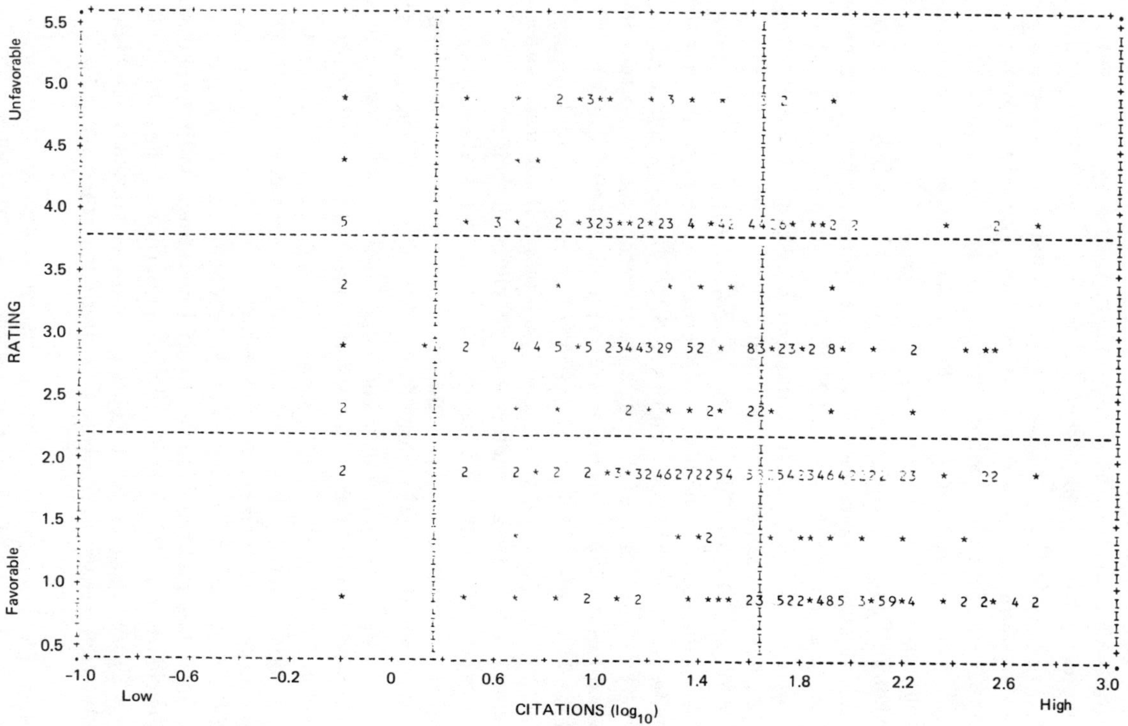

FIGURE 4 Log of citations in 1974 to papers published from 1965 to 1974 and peer review ratings: biochemistry. (Note: An asterisk in the scattergram represents one case; numbers 2-8 represent that number of cases; a 9 represents nine or more cases at that point on the scattergram.)

CITATIONS ($\log_{10}$)

RATING

Unfavorable

Favorable

Low

High

received relatively low (read high) ratings on their proposals. In other words, there is substantial overlap in the ratings received by highly cited scientists and those with few citations. Thus it is impossible to predict accurately the rating a scientist's proposal will get from knowledge of the number of citations to the recent work of that scientist.

We illustrate further the lack of a relationship between citations to recent work and peer review ratings by considering the results obtained for 2 of the 10 programs: biochemistry, in which the association between these 2 variables was highest among the 10 programs, and ecology, which had the second lowest association. Figure 4 presents the scattergram for the relationship between citations to recent work and ratings received in biochemistry. Again, a great number of scientists whose recent work has received a substantial number of citations obtained relatively poor peer review ratings. Correlatively, many scientists who have received few citations to their recent work obtained very good or excellent peer review ratings, represented by "low" scores on the NSF rating scale. In short, this scattergram suggests that the association between these two variables is relatively weak. This is even more apparent when we examine Figure 5, in which we present the same relationship for applicants to the ecology program. Here we see almost no relationship between these two variables.

Thus far we have used two analytic techniques to explore the possibility that a scientist's past track record is associated with peer review ratings. At least for this one indicator of track record, we have concluded that there is no substantial relationship between ratings and citations to recent work. In fact, using simple regression models we find a very pronounced lack of fit between the data and the model. Examination of the scattergrams suggests why the regression model does not provide a good description of the relationship between citations to recent work and peer review ratings. It is unlikely that any simple function could describe the data presented here.

Now we compare the results obtained from regression and scattergram analyses with those obtained from tabular analysis of the same data. In Table 17 we show the relationship between the number of citations received in 1974 to work published between 1965 and 1974 and the rating received on the proposal. For purposes of tabular analysis we have dichotomized ratings into excellent or very good (the two highest rating categories), and all others. Thus, within each program we show for each citation category the proportion of applicants who received excellent or very good ratings. For example, in 134 cases in algebra the applicant had no citations. In 63 percent of these cases the applicant received a rating of excellent or very good. In tabular

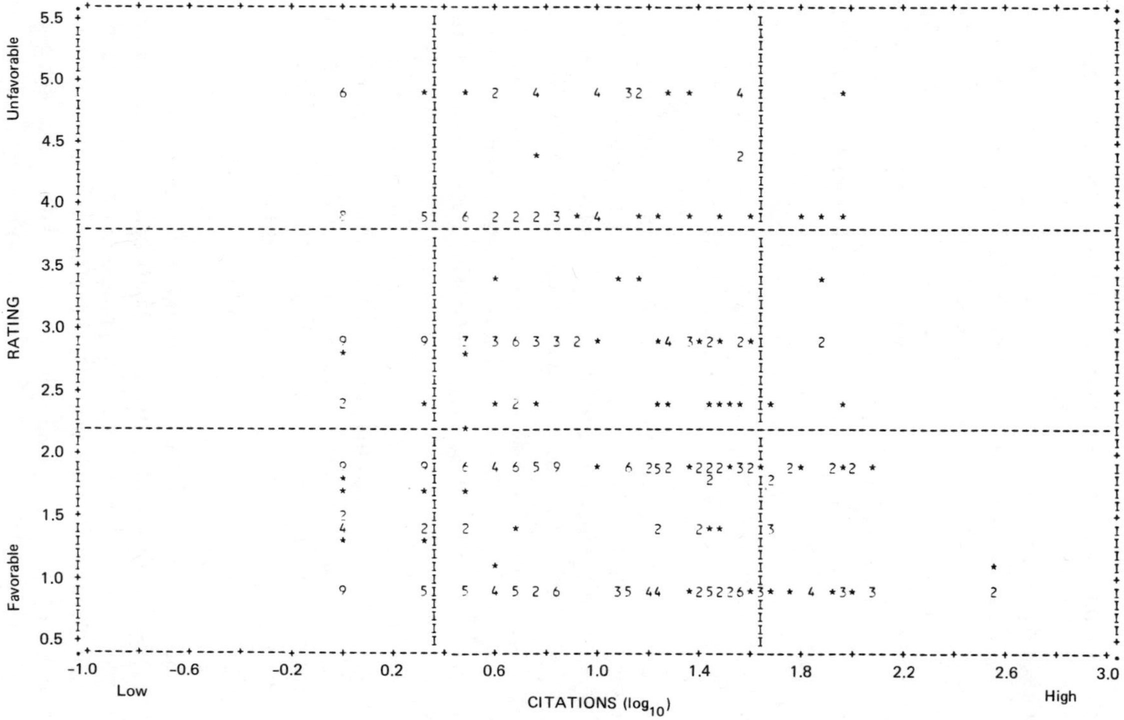

FIGURE 5 Log of citations in 1974 to papers published from 1965 to 1974 and peer review ratings: ecology. (Note: An asterisk in the scattergram represents one case; numbers 2-8 represent that number of cases; a 9 represents nine or more cases at that point on the scattergram.)

58

TABLE 17 Applicants Receiving Excellent or Very Good Ratings by Citations in 1974 to Work Published Between 1965 and 1974: 10 Programs

Number of Citations	Algebra, %	Number of Citations	Anthropology, %	Number of Citations	Biochemistry, %	Number of Citations	Chemical Dynamics, %	Number of Citations	Ecology, %
0	63 (134)	0	51 (86)	0-10	23 (79)	0-11	42 (72)	0-1	65 (85)
1-3	65 (49)	1-2	46 (63)	11-22	37 (91)	12-29	49 (78)	2-4	54 (82)
4-8	72 (75)	3-6	64 (36)	23-45	45 (83)	30-56	65 (81)	5-7	59 (66)
9 or more	88 (57)	7 or more	52 (42)	46-83	61 (85)	57-81	76 (70)	8-26	54 (77)
				84 or more	80 (85)	82 or more	82 (91)	27 or more	71 (92)

Number of Citations	Economics, %	Number of Citations	Fluid Mechanics, %	Number of Citations	Geophysics, %	Number of Citations	Meteorology, %	Number of Citations	Solid-State Physics, %
0	37 (90)	0	42 (67)	0-2	52 (99)	0-1	31 (132)	0-4	48 (103)
1	37 (35)	1-2	46 (35)	3-8	43 (98)	2-4	26 (81)	5-16	67 (112)
2-5	56 (78)	3-6	44 (81)	9-19	57 (102)	5-9	32 (111)	17-33	65 (94)
6-14	58 (59)	7-12	40 (65)	20-41	70 (91)	10-22	49 (122)	34-72	67 (100)
15 or more	68 (62)	13 or more	60 (87)	42 or more	76 (101)	23 or more	60 (116)	73 or more	83 (89)

Numbers of applicants are in parentheses.

analysis it is also necessary to categorize the independent variable, citations. We have done this by dividing up the cases within each field roughly into quintiles. Table 17 shows that in every field, scientists who have received the most citations for that field were more likely to get an excellent or very good rating on the proposal than those who were in the lowest citation category.[9] The percentage difference between high and low varies considerably from one field to another. For example, in anthropology, 51 percent of applicants in the lowest citation category received excellent or very good ratings, whereas 52 percent of those in the highest citation category received excellent or very good ratings. Biochemistry, the field in which the regression analysis indicated citations had the largest effect on ratings, shows the largest percentage difference. Twenty-three percent of those in the lowest citation category as compared with 80 percent of those in the highest citation category received excellent or very good ratings on their proposals.

The data presented in Table 17 can be used to provide answers to both of the questions we are concerned with in this section. We have already used regression and scattergram techniques in addressing the first question: To what extent can we predict the ratings of a proposal from knowledge of the number of citations to the applicant's recent work? We conclude from the tabular analysis that in the majority of fields, citations are of little or no use in predicting ratings.[10]

---

[9] It has been suggested that we should have drawn the dichotomy between "excellent" and all other ratings. When this was done, the results obtained in percentage differences were virtually identical with those reported in Table 17.

[10] The reader will note that we do not present tests of statistical significance for most of the tables appearing in this report. Many of the relationships shown in the tables are statistically significant. However, the reader should be aware of the difference between statistical and substantive significance. If a relationship is *statistically* significant, there is a very low probability that the percentage difference observed would be obtained by chance if there were not a real difference between groups in the population. However, statistical significance does not indicate the size or substantive significance of the difference between groups. In many of the tables that we have presented, there is a statistically significant difference, meaning that the difference displayed is unlikely to be a result of chance but nonetheless of little substantive meaning because of the small size of the difference. There is no precise way to determine whether or not a percentage difference of a particular size is substantively significant. There has been a continuing debate among sociologists for the last 20 years over the value of statistical tests of significance. (See Denton E. Morrison and Ramon E. Henkel, eds., *The Significance Test Controversy*.) This controversy is of no concern to us here. Our position here is simple: We have used these tests where we believe they add to our substantive understanding of the NSF peer review system, for example, in the analysis of variance conducted in section 2.

Solid-state physics is a field in which the relationship between citations and ratings is moderate: a total of 65 percent of the 495 ratings were either excellent or very good. If we have to guess whether or not a particular scientist would get an excellent or a very good rating, and we knew nothing else about that scientist or about his or her proposal, we would guess that he or she had a high rating and be correct in 65 percent of the cases. To what extent is this 65 percent correct prediction rate improved by knowledge of the number of citations to the applicant's recent work? The data on solid-state physics in Table 17 show that among the applicants in the lowest citation category, only 48 percent received high ratings. We would, therefore, predict that all these people would receive low ratings. We would be correct 52 percent of the time, or in 54 cases; we would be incorrect in 49 cases. In the next citation category, 67 percent of the applicants received high ratings. We would, therefore, predict that all these applicants would receive high ratings; correct in 75 cases and incorrect in 37 cases. The same arithmetic for the bottom three categories, using the number of citations received to predict rating, would give 330 correct cases and 165 incorrect cases. The proportion that we guessed correctly would be 67 percent, or only 2 percent better than what we could have done by chance without any knowledge of citations.[11]

Similar demonstrations could be done for the data on all the other fields. Biochemistry is the field in which citations have the greatest influence on ratings; they add more to our ability to predict ratings. In this field, citations enable us to predict 67 percent of the cases correctly, an increase of 17 percent over what we would have predicted by chance without any knowledge of citation. Our point here is that even though number of citations an applicant has received shows a moderate relationship with rating, citations do not add significantly to our ability to predict whether or not a particular applicant would get a high or low rating. We come to this conclusion using either tabular or regression analysis. However, we can answer a question using tabular analysis that we can't answer by regression analysis, namely: what are the conditional probabilities of receiving high ratings for scientists who differ greatly in their track records or in other characteristics we have been considering? With the tabular analysis it is possible to compare people who are at the extremes of a distribution. For example, in the programs of chemical dynamics, economics, and meteorology, applicants in the highest citation category are almost twice as likely to receive excellent or very good ratings as applicants in the lowest

---

[11]This is roughly equivalent to computing a lambda statistic.

citation category. However, in anthropology and ecology, there is practically no difference between the highest and lowest citation categories.

The data for the fluid mechanics program show us how the tabular data permit us to address more detailed questions than those accessible in a simple regression analysis. (See Table 17.) If we compare the fluid mechanics applicants in the lowest citation category with those in the highest citation category, we find a 20 percent difference, that is, 40 percent of applicants in fluid mechanics received no citations to their work and 60 percent of applicants in the highest citation category received either excellent or very good ratings on their proposals. These figures tell us the difference between people at the two extremes of the citation distribution. They do not tell us the extent to which the number of citations received is a good *predictor* of ratings *among all applicants* to the fluid mechanics program. In fact, if we examine the proportion receiving excellent or very good ratings on their proposals across the entire distribution of citations we find that for 80 percent of applicants in fluid mechanics, those in the first four quintiles, there is no difference whatsoever in the proportion receiving excellent or very good ratings. The only category in which there is a difference is the top category, those receiving 13 or more citations. Since citations explain no variance in rating among 80 percent of the sample, the overall predictability of ratings from citations in this field is very low.

A similar finding can be observed for solid-state physics. If we compare people in the lowest citation category with those in the highest citation category, we find a 36 percent difference. However, when we examine the 60 percent of all the applicants who fall in the three middle categories we find no difference at all in the proportion receiving excellent or very good ratings. Thus, on 60 percent of the sample in solid-state physics, citations are of no use in predicting ratings; therefore, the overall predictability of ratings from citations will be low. But, the tabular analysis shows that those scientists in the lowest citation category, at an extreme in the distribution, have a lower probability of receiving high ratings and those scientists in the top citation category, at the other extreme of the distribution, have a considerably higher probability of receiving favorable ratings on their proposals.

Table 18 presents the proportion of variance on ratings explained by citations made in 1974 to work published prior to 1965. Here we find a positive but very weak relationship in all 10 fields. Substantively, this means that scientists who are well known as a result of work published more than 10 years ago are only slightly more likely to get higher ratings than scientists who are not well known on the basis of work

TABLE 18 Proportion of Variance
Explained (R^2) on Rating by Citations
to Old Work: 10 Programs[a]

Algebra	0.03
Anthropology	0.02
Biochemistry	0.06
Chemical Dynamics	0.05
Ecology	0.01
Economics	0.02
Fluid Mechanics	0.07
Geophysics	0.02
Meteorology	0.01
Solid-State Physics	0.03

[a]Log of citations made in 1974 to work
published prior to 1965.

published 10 or more years ago. When we use the standardized data for all 10 programs combined, we find that the citations to older work explain only 2 percent of the variance on rating. The tabular data on this variable are presented in Table 19.

Table 20 presents the proportion of variance explained on ratings by the numbers of papers published in the last 10 years. In 4 of the 10 programs (algebra, anthropology, ecology, and economics) no variance is explained. The number of papers published explains only 1 percent of variance in ratings in fluid mechanics, 7 percent for biochemistry, 9 percent for chemical dynamics, and 12 percent for meteorology. When we use the standardized data for all 10 programs combined, we find that the number of papers published in 1965-1974 explains 2 percent of the variance in ratings.

It is worth noting that there are generally high correlations between the number of papers a scientist has published and the number of times that he or she has been cited. In fact, in biochemistry, the field that on the average shows the highest correlation between the three productivity variables and the ratings, we found that all three variables together explained only 17 percent of the variance, only 1 percent more than was explained by citations to recent work.

Table 21 presents the relationship between the total number of papers published between 1965 and 1974 and ratings received by applicants in each of the 10 fields. In 7 of the 10 programs there is less than a 20 percent point difference between scientists who have published no papers and those who have published the most papers in the proportion of applicants receiving excellent or very good ratings on

TABLE 19 Applicants Receiving Excellent or Very Good Ratings by Citations in 1974 to Work Published Prior to 1965: 10 Programs

Number of Citations	Algebra, %	Number of Citations	Anthropology, %	Number of Citations	Biochemistry, %	Number of Citations	Chemical Dynamics, %	Number of Citations	Ecology, %
0	69 (266)	0	50 (188)	0	42 (171)	0	58 (218)	0	59 (261)
1 or more	76 (49)	1 or more	59 (39)	1-6	45 (124)	1-18	64 (101)	1 or more	64 (141)
				7 or more	64 (128)	19 or more	78 (73)		

Number of Citations	Economics, %	Number of Citations	Fluid Mechanics, %	Number of Citations	Geophysics, %	Number of Citations	Meteorology, %	Number of Citations	Solid-State Physics, %
0	49 (254)	0	43 (188)	0	55 (313)	0	39 (350)	0	61 (241)
1 or more	59 (70)	1 or more	52 (147)	1,2	65 (46)	1,2	41 (117)	1-12	67 (150)
				3 or more	70 (132)	3 or more	47 (95)	13 or more	74 (107)

Numbers of applicants are in parentheses.

64

TABLE 20 Proportion of Variance
Explained (R^2) on Rating by Papers
Published between 1965 and 1974:
10 Programs[a]

Algebra	0.00
Anthropology	0.00
Biochemistry	0.07
Chemical Dynamics	0.09
Ecology	0.00
Economics	0.00
Fluid Mechanics	0.01
Geophysics	0.04
Meteorology	0.12
Solid-State Physics	0.04

[a] A log transformation has been used.

their proposals. The exceptions are biochemistry (35 percent), fluid mechanics (26 percent), and chemical dynamics (30 percent). Note that in ecology those scientists who have published the most papers are less apt to get favorable ratings on their proposals than those who have published the least papers, and in economics there is no difference between the extreme publication categories.

It is clear that our prior expectations as to which scientists would be most likely to get high ratings on their proposals are only weakly supported by the data. If reviewers are being influenced at all by the past performances and reputations of principal investigators, the influence is not great.

These data also lead to another, more puzzling, conclusion—that there will be a low-to-moderate correlation between the perceived quality of the science in proposals submitted and the past performances of the principal investigators as indicated by published papers and citations. This conclusion is indicated because if there were a high correlation between the perceived quality of proposals and the characteristics of their authors, we would then expect to find a higher correlation between the characteristics of authors and the ratings received. There are two possibilities. One, reviewers could be basing their ratings predominantly on their perception of the quality of the science in the proposals. In this case there would be only a moderate correlation between reviewers' perceptions of the quality of the science and the past performances of the principal investigators. Two, there could be a great deal of disagreement among reviewers. (See

TABLE 21 Applicants Receiving Excellent or Very Good Ratings by Number of Papers Published Between 1965 and 1974: 10 Programs

Number of Papers	Algebra, %	Number of Papers	Anthropology, %	Number of Papers	Biochemistry, %	Number of Papers	Chemical Dynamics, %	Number of Papers	Ecology, %
0-2	63 (68)	0-1	54 (56)	0-9	30 (80)	0-11	44 (77)	0,1,2	76 (75)
3-7	78 (85)	2-14	44 (70)	10-16	42 (87)	12-18	61 (72)	3,4,5	50 (92)
8-13	61 (77)	15-35	51 (45)	17-25	46 (83)	19-29	71 (82)	6-11	60 (75)
14 or more	75 (85)	36 or more	61 (56)	26-46	62 (87)	30-48	65 (75)	12-18	53 (66)
				47 or more	65 (86)	49 or more	74 (86)	19 or more	66 (94)

Number of Papers	Economics, %	Number of Papers	Fluid Mechanics, %	Number of Papers	Geophysics, %	Number of Papers	Meteorology, %	Number of Papers	Solid-State Physics, %
0-1	49 (86)	0-2	41 (59)	0-4	48 (96)	0-3	33 (120)	0-9	51 (106)
2-15	53 (83)	3-9	50 (91)	5-10	50 (91)	4-9	24 (94)	10-17	72 (101)
16-51	53 (75)	10-19	34 (74)	11-20	54 (106)	10-15	44 (128)	18-25	70 (98)
52 or more	50 (80)	20 or more	57 (111)	21-31	70 (91)	16-27	46 (107)	26-44	70 (90)
				32 or more	75 (107)	28 or more	52 (113)	45 or more	65 (103)

Numbers of applicants are in parentheses.

discussion at end of this section.) The reviewing process could contain a large arbitrary element. If this is the case, we will find a low correlation between ratings given by the NSF reviewers and ratings given by independently chosen sets of reviewers. Phase 2 of this research project, which is currently under way, will investigate this possibility.

We are concerned with one other variable as an indicator of the past track records of principal investigators—the number of years out of the last 5 in which they have received NSF funds. Some applicants had received NSF funds in all or several of the years, whereas others had received NSF funds in none of those 5 years. Do applicants who currently are or recently have been NSF grant recipients have a greater likelihood of getting favorable ratings from reviewers? The data in Table 22 indicate that whether or not applicants are recent past recipients of NSF funds has very little influence on ratings of their current applications. In all 10 programs the proportion of variance explained by funding history is low. In one program it is 0, in two others it is 1 percent of the variance, and in two others it is only 2 percent of the variance. The greatest proportion of variance explained is in economics, but even here only 8 percent of the variance is explained by funding histories of applicants. When we use the standardized data for all 10 programs combined, we find that NSF funding history explains 3 percent of the variance on rating. Again, we conclude that recent NSF funding history has relatively little influence on the ratings received.

In Figure 6 we present a scattergram displaying the relationship between the funding history of applicants and ratings received on their current proposals. For this scattergram we have used the combined sample of standardized data for all 10 programs. As we would expect

TABLE 22 Proportion of Variance Explained (R^2) on Rating by Years Funded: 1970-1974

Algebra	0.05
Anthropology	0.00
Biochemistry	0.06
Chemical Dynamics	0.05
Ecology	0.02
Economics	0.08
Fluid Mechanics	0.01
Geophysics	0.01
Meteorology	0.02
Solid-State Physics	0.06

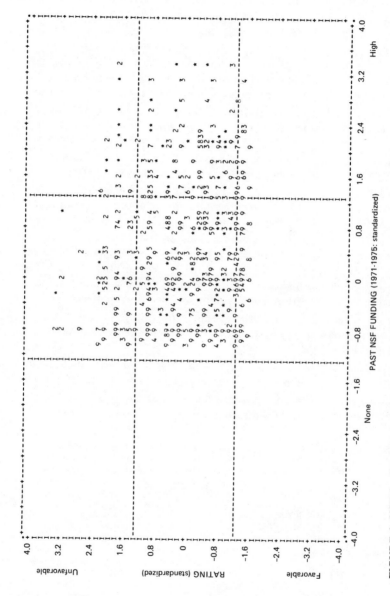

FIGURE 6 NSF funding history (1971-1975) and standardized peer review ratings: all 10 fields. (Note: An asterisk in the scattergram represents one case; numbers 2-8 represent that number of cases; a 9 represents nine or more cases at that point on the scattergram.)

68

from the previous associations just reported, the scattergram shows that there is no significant association between the two variables. Many applicants who have received no NSF funding in the last 5 years received favorable ratings on their proposals, and many applicants who have been funded during the entire period received unfavorable ratings on their proposals. In short, knowledge of whether or not an applicant has been funded by the NSF in the recent past is of little or no use in predicting the rating of a current proposal. It is clear from the cloud of points presented in Figure 6 why the regression results of Table 22 show no significant association between granting history and ratings received.

Table 23 shows the relationship between granting history and ratings received, using tabular analysis. For the tabular analysis we have dichotomized the applicants into those who have and those who have not received NSF funds in the last 5 years. In one program, anthropology, applicants who recently received NSF funds actually had a slightly lower probability of getting excellent or very good ratings on their proposals than did applicants who had not received NSF funds in the last 5 years. In all the other nine programs the differences between the two groups of applicants in the proportion receiving excellent or very good ratings were only slight to moderate but are definitely worth noting. The field showing the strongest relationship was economics. In this field, 73 percent of past NSF grantees and 42 percent of those who had not received NSF funds received excellent or very good ratings on their proposals.

TABLE 23 Applicants Receiving Excellent or Very Good Ratings by Past Funding History: 10 Programs

Program	Received NSF Funds in Last 5 Years, %		Did Not Receive NSF Funds in Last 5 Years, %	
Algebra	74	(152)	66	(131)
Anthropology	48	(48)	53	(169)
Biochemistry	58	(248)	37	(172)
Chemical Dynamics	74	(166)	56	(187)
Ecology	67	(181)	55	(204)
Economics	73	(95)	42	(214)
Fluid Mechanics	51	(174)	44	(151)
Geophysics	64	(297)	53	(161)
Meteorology	45	(295)	34	(232)
Solid-State Physics	76	(225)	57	(267)

Numbers of applicants are in parentheses.

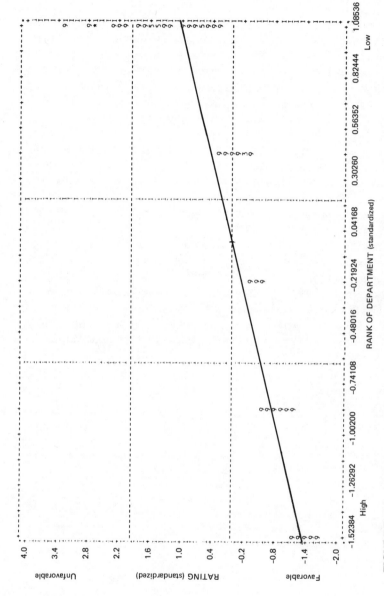

FIGURE 7 Maximum association between peer review ratings and rank of applicant's current department. (Note: An asterisk in the scattergram represents one case; numbers 2-8 represent that number of cases; a 9 represents nine or more cases at that point on the scattergram.)

LOCATION AT PRESTIGIOUS DEPARTMENTS AND PEER REVIEW RATINGS

Our data also tell us whether peer reviewers are more likely to give favorable ratings to scientists in the most prestigious academic departments. We might expect to find such a correlation, since presumably some departments are more highly ranked than others because they have more superior scientists in them. These scientists should get higher ratings both because of their capabilities as scientists and because it is presumed that their research proposals are better. As the data in Table 24 show, however, there is not a strong correlation between the rank of an applicant's current department and the rating he receives from peer reviewers. In all the programs, with the exception of anthropology, there is a correlation between the rank of applicants' departments and the ratings given their proposals; but again these correlations are surprisingly low. The greatest proportion of variance explained by department rankings is in economics, but even here only 13 percent of the variance is explained by department ranking. These data lead to the conclusion that reviewers are not being significantly influenced by the affiliations of applicants. They are only slightly more apt to give higher ratings to applicants from prestigious institutions than to those from less prestigious institutions. When we use the standardized data for all 10 programs combined, we find that rank of current department explains 5 percent of the variance in ratings.

Figure 7 shows what the relationship would be between the rank of an applicant's department and the applicant's rating if there were a

TABLE 24 Proportion of Variance Explained (R^2) on Rating by Rank of Present Department

Algebra	0.07
Anthropology	0.00
Biochemistry	0.07
Chemical Dynamics	0.02
Ecology	0.02
Economics	0.13
Fluid Mechanics	0.10
Geophysics[a]	0.03
Meteorology[a]	0.05
Solid-State Physics	0.08

[a]Rank of department scores based upon survey of NAS members (see Appendix B).

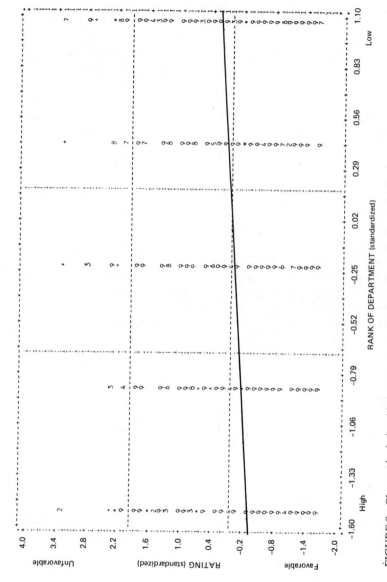

FIGURE 8 Observed relationship between peer review ratings and rank of applicant's current department. (Note: An asterisk in the scattergram represents one case; numbers 2–8 represent that number of cases; a 9 represents nine or more cases at that point on the scattergram.)

perfect or maximum association between these two variables. For this illustration we use the standardized data from the combined sample. We have roughly drawn in the least-squares regression line. The slope is 0.904. (Since the data are standardized, the correlation coefficient is equal to the slope.) Even if there were a "perfect" relationship between rating and rank of department, we would not get a correlation coefficient of 1 because rank of department is not a continuous variable. (We divided departments into five categories.) If all the highest ratings were assigned to the applicants from the highest-rank departments, only 82 percent of the variance in ratings would be explained.

The actual distribution of the data is presented in Figure 8. The slope, or the correlation coefficient, for this regression line is 0.213. Thus, the rank of an applicant's department explains only about 0.045 percent of the variance on ratings; the regression equation is an inadequate predictor of an applicant's rating. Examining the extent to which the points in the scattergram are spread out both above and below the regression line and the tremendous amount of overlap in the rating scores for people in departments of different rank emphasizes our point. Table 25 shows the relationship between the rank of an applicant's current department and the ratings received on the proposal. With the exception of anthropology, scientists who come from the highest-ranked departments are indeed more likely to receive higher ratings than those who come from unranked or nonacademic departments. However, in several of the programs, such as chemical dynamics, ecology, and geophysics, this relationship is very weak. In several of the programs the relationship is nonlinear. For example, in chemical dynamics, 78 percent of scientists from the highest-ranked departments received high ratings, 67 percent of those in the next group received high ratings, but 78 percent of those in the fourth group received high ratings—the same proportion as that received by scientists in the highest-ranked departments. Other fields show a similar lack of linearity. For example, in solid-state physics, scientists located in the lowest-ranked departments received just about the same proportion of high ratings as those in the most prestigious departments.

These findings on the relationship between rank of department and ratings seem to contradict common sense. On closer examination, however, they corroborate the findings of prior empirical studies in the sociology of science. Although it is true that, *on the average,* highly prestigious departments have more productive and talented scientists, a non-negligible proportion of talented scientists are not in the most prestigious departments. Several independent studies have found that the correlation between citations to a scientist's work and the prestige

TABLE 25 Applicants Receiving Excellent or Very Good Ratings by Rank of Current Department: 10 Programs

Program	1 Current Department Ranked High, %		2 Current Department Ranked Medium, %		3 Current Department Ranked Medium, %		4 Current Department Ranked Low, %		5 Current Department Unranked or Nonacademic, %	
Algebra	87	(23)	81	(52)	76	(71)	63	(38)	61	(131)
Anthropology	50	(24)	47	(34)	30	(10)	70	(20)	53	(139)
Biochemistry	80	(46)	68	(40)	61	(23)	33	(33)	43	(281)
Chemical Dynamics	78	(37)	67	(27)	65	(86)	78	(77)	51	(167)
Ecology	67	(104)	71	(45)	64	(22)	59	(69)	54	(162)
Economics	76	(85)	60	(57)	53	(30)	0	(13)	37	(139)
Fluid Mechanics	70	(98)	51	(61)	42	(40)	28	(50)	31	(86)
Geophysics[a]	72	(97)	64	(47)	56	(171)	55	(146)	60	(30)
Meteorology[a]	57	(122)	44	(110)	41	(95)	30	(131)	32	(104)
Solid-State Physics	81	(145)	67	(54)	71	(76)	78	(9)	52	(214)

Numbers of applicants are in parentheses.

[a]Rank of department scores based upon survey of NAS members (see Appendix B).

74

rank of his department is 0.30 or less. (For a review of the literature on this topic see Cole and Zuckerman, 1976.) This means that quite a few scientists who have produced high-quality work are not in highly ranked departments.

When we relate the low correlation between the quality of an individual scientist's research output and the rank of his department to the concept of self-selection we can understand better the low correlation between the rank of an applicant's department and peer review ratings. If every scientist in every department applied for a grant, there would probably be a considerably higher correlation between rank of department and rating. But we know that all scientists do not apply. Applying scientists from low-ranked departments are probably the most active researchers. Whereas six mathematicians from MIT may apply for NSF funds in a given year, perhaps only one mathematician at a lower-ranked department will apply. But this one man will possibly have a national reputation comparable to those of some of his colleagues at higher-ranked departments. The relatively wide dispersion of scientific talent and the process of self-selection may well provide the explanation of the data in Table 25.

To illustrate how tabular analysis allows us to compare people at the extremes of a distribution, we have computed an index in which applicants are given scores based upon the quintiles of their citations and the quintile ranks of their current departments. A scientist in the highest-ranked department with the highest number of citations would receive a score of 10. A scientist in the lowest-ranked department with the lowest number of citations would receive a score of 2. Table 26 shows the proportion of applicants in each index category who received excellent or very good ratings. Thirty-four percent of those in the lowest index category and 80 percent of those in the highest category received excellent or very good ratings. Since 56 percent of all the ratings were very good or excellent, we could predict 56 percent correctly by chance. Using this index composed of the two independent variables that had the strongest effect on the dependent variable

TABLE 26 Applicants Receiving Excellent or Very Good Ratings by Index of Citations and Rank of Department: All Fields Combined[a]

2	3	4	5	6	7	8	9	10
34%	43%	51%	50%	56%	61%	68%	75%	80%
(294)	(425)	(482)	(646)	(561)	(485)	(326)	(320)	(230)

The first row of numbers indicates index scores. Numbers of applicants are in parentheses.
[a]Rank of department was broken down into quintiles using the Z scores.

rating, we were able to increase the number of cases we could predict correctly to 60 percent. This suggests still further that our ability to predict ratings from these independent variables is not greatly enhanced by constructing such indices. One reason why the overall predictability is not greater is that there are relatively few cases in these extremes. For example, only 6 percent of all the cases are in the highest index category and only 8 percent of all the cases are in the lowest. A great majority of the cases are in the middle index categories between 4 and 7, where the percentage difference is only 10 points. Since this distribution is not artifactual but is representative of the distribution of the scientists who applied to the 10 programs we studied at the NSF, it cannot be discounted. Since there is not a great deal of variance in the independent variables, they are of little use in making better predictions of the dependent variable. This is one reason why citations are not a strong predictor of ratings in algebra, fluid mechanics, anthropology, and economics.

However, the data displayed in Table 26 also allow us to compare scientists who are at different ends of the index combining citations and rank of department. Let us compare the probabilities of receiving excellent or very good ratings among scientists at the two extremes. Table 26 shows a 46 percentage point difference between the two groups. This substantial difference in probability does not contradict our findings of overall low predictability because we are dealing with only 14 percent of the total sample. Table 26 shows, as one would expect and hope, that scientists with a very high index are much more likely to receive high ratings than those with a very low index. However, the number of scientists between the two extremes is so large that the index has very little predictive value.

TABLE 27 Proportion of Variance Explained (R^2) on Rating by Type of Current Institution (Ph.D. or not): 10 Programs

Algebra	0.01
Anthropology	0.01
Biochemistry	0.02
Chemical Dynamics	0.00
Ecology	0.04
Economics	0.07
Fluid Mechanics	0.01
Geophysics	0.04
Meteorology	0.02
Solid-State Physics	0.01

TABLE 28   Proportion of Variance Explained
(R^2) on Rating by Rank of Ph.D. Department

Algebra	0.04
Anthropology	0.02
Biochemistry	0.02
Chemical Dynamics	0.04
Ecology	0.01[a]
Economics	0.03
Fluid Mechanics	0.00
Geophysics[b]	0.02
Meteorology[b]	0.02
Solid-State Physics	0.02

[a]Relationship is negative.
[b]Rank of department scores based upon survey of
NAS members (see Appendix B).

The data in Table 27 distinguish applicants currently employed in
Ph.D.-granting institutions from those employed elsewhere. This has
virtually no influence on ratings of proposals by peer reviewers. Thus
the criticisms that the peer review system unfairly favors applicants
from prestigious Ph.D.-granting institutions are not supported by these
data.

The data on the rankings of the departments in which the applicants
earned their Ph.D's showed the extent to which this variable was
correlated with ratings given by peer reviewers. Table 28 shows that
the rankings of Ph.D. departments of applicants explain very little
variance in ratings received.

PROFESSIONAL AGE AND PEER REVIEW RATINGS

Some critics of the peer review system hold that young, inexperienced
applicants have less chance to receive funds than their more experienced older colleagues. We have data on the ages of applicants and on
the numbers of years since applicants received their Ph.D.'s, which we
call their professional age. The results of this analysis are presented in
Table 29. The findings are clear. In five of the programs professional
age explains no variance in the ratings given by peer reviewers. In four
programs professional age explained only 1 percent of the variance in
ratings. These data strongly suggest that young people have just as
good a chance to receive favorable ratings of their proposals as do their
older, more experienced colleagues. This conclusion is supported by

TABLE 29 Proportion of Variance Explained
(R^2) on Rating by Professional Age[a]

Algebra	0.00
Anthropology	0.00
Biochemistry	0.01
Chemical Dynamics	0.01
Ecology	0.00
Economics	0.00
Fluid Mechanics	0.01
Geophysics	0.01
Meteorology	0.00
Solid-State Physics	0.03

[a]Professional age was divided into two classes—those
who received Ph.D.'s in the last 5 years and those who
received Ph.D.'s more than 5 years ago.

the results reported in Table 30, which shows the influence of academic
rank (only for those employed in academic institutions) of applicants
on ratings received. A high correlation would indicate that applicants
with high academic rank have a better chance of getting favorable
ratings than applicants of lower rank. Once again, the proportions of
explained variance are either nonexistent or very small. Apparently,
full professors do not have a significantly better chance than their
lower-ranked colleagues.

Table 31 presents the relationship between professional age and
ratings received for each of the 10 programs, using tabular analysis. In
algebra, ecology, and meteorology, applicants who have received their
Ph.D.'s within the last 5 years have slightly higher probabilities of
receiving excellent or very good ratings than do applicants who re-

TABLE 30 Proportion of Variance Explained
(R^2) on Rating by Academic Rank

Algebra	0.03
Anthropology	0.00
Biochemistry	0.02
Chemical Dynamics	0.00
Ecology	0.00
Economics	0.03
Fluid Mechanics	0.01
Geophysics	0.00
Meteorology	0.00
Solid-State Physics	0.03

TABLE 31 Applicants Receiving Excellent or Very Good Ratings by
Professional Age

Program	Received Ph.D. More Than 5 Years Ago, %		Received Ph.D. within the Last 5 Years, %	
Algebra	68	(213)	76	(70)
Anthropology	54	(123)	51	(85)
Biochemistry	51	(359)	43	(61)
Chemical Dynamics	66	(293)	57	(60)
Ecology	61	(264)	63	(115)
Economics	52	(181)	48	(92)
Fluid Mechanics	50	(267)	38	(39)
Geophysics	62	(348)	56	(104)
Meteorology	40	(392)	42	(98)
Solid-State Physics	69	(421)	49	(59)

Numbers of applicants are in parentheses.

ceived their Ph.D.'s more than 5 years ago. In most of the other programs the difference in the proportion receiving excellent or very good ratings between relatively new Ph.D.'s and older Ph.D.'s is slight. The one program that shows a moderate relationship between these two variables is solid-state physics. Sixty-nine percent of scientists who received their Ph.D.'s more than 5 years ago received excellent or very good ratings, and 49 percent of those who received their Ph.D.'s within the last 5 years received excellent or very good ratings.

COMBINING THE NINE CHARACTERISTICS

We conclude our analysis of the influence of principal investigators' characteristics on reviewer ratings with Table 32. This table presents the amount of variance explained in ratings by all nine characteristics of applicants, using multiple regression analysis. The table shows that the characteristics of principal investigators on whom we have data explain only a small portion of the variance in ratings in all 10 programs.

Economics is the program in which the largest proportion of variance in ratings—21 percent—is explained by the combination of nine characteristics of the principal investigators. We should point out that we do not know the extent to which even this variance in ratings is a result of the influence of these nine characteristics of applicants and how much is due to an unknown correlation between the characteristics of appli-

TABLE 32 Proportion of Variance Explained on Ratings Given by All Nine Characteristics of Principal Investigators (10 Variable Regression Equations[a] for Each Program)

Program	Proportion of Variance Explained in Each Program, Multiple R^2
Algebra	0.17
Anthropology	0.04
Biochemistry	0.20
Chemical Dynamics	0.16
Ecology	0.06
Economics	0.21
Fluid Mechanics	0.17
Geophysics	0.09
Meteorology	0.14
Solid-State Physics	0.17
All 10 programs combined (standardized data)	0.11

[a]If an independent variable had a "negative" correlation with rating (i.e., eminent scientists being less likely than noneminent scientists to receive favorable ratings), the variable was omitted from the multiple regression equation for that program. The omitted variables were as follows: anthropology (rank of current department and NSF funding history), ecology (number of published papers, rank of Ph.D. department, and professional age).

cants we have been studying and the quality of their proposals. It probably involves some combination of these two factors. We tentatively conclude that a significant portion of the variance in these ratings is either a result of the perception of the quality of proposals or of a random grading process. The data we are collecting in Phase 2 of this research project may shed additional light on this important issue.

From the data presented in this section we can draw two conclusions. (1) *On the average,* the nine characteristics of principal investigators that we have studied have little effect on the ratings of their proposals. (2) The scientists at the extremes of the distribution, the very highly cited and the noncited, have significantly different probabilities of receiving excellent or very good ratings. To reiterate, the tabular data show that scientists with the most citations among applicants to their programs are substantially more likely to receive favorable ratings on their proposals than those with few or no citations. The reason why this difference between the extremes does not produce greater correlations and, therefore, explain greater amounts of variance is that relatively small numbers of scientists are at the extremes. Furthermore, the relatively small size of our samples prevents us from examining in greater detail the ratings received by the most eminent applicants to particular programs. If we were to look at the top 1 or 2 percent of applicants to NSF programs, for instance, we might find that they almost invariably do get high ratings on their proposals. Further research is needed on how the proposals of the small number of extraordinarily eminent scientists fare in the National Science Foundation peer review system.

SIGNIFICANCE OF FINDINGS

The fact that the nine characteristics explain so little variance in ratings is contrary to the expectations of many people. We must therefore consider carefully the significance of our data. First, let us consider a possible error in the methodology. We have used applicant and reviewer as the unit of analysis. Applicants who had many reviewers, of course, appeared more often than those who had fewer reviewers. It is possible that there would be less agreement among reviewers on proposals that had a large number of reviewers, since program directors typically request additional reviewers when there is disagreement among the initial set. If cases on which there is disagreement are over-represented in the sample, the correlations are artificially reduced.

Indeed, it turns out that for most of the 10 programs there is a negative correlation between the amount of agreement among the reviewers of a proposal (as measured by the variance of the ratings) and the number of reviewers of the proposal. This correlation ranged between $r = 0.00$ for chemical dynamics and $r = -0.51$ for economics. To see if this correlation had any significant influence on the results reported in the tables presented in this section, we performed an experiment in the field of ecology. We chose this program because it showed a relatively high negative correlation between degree of agreement among reviewers and the number of reviewers ($r = -0.44$) and a low correlation between citations to recent work and ratings ($R^2 = 0.01$).

We divided the ecology applicants into those who had three or fewer reviewers and those who had four or more. We then ran regression equations separately in each group. If the correlations were being reduced by over-representation of applicants with large numbers of reviewers and a low level of agreement, then the proportion of explained variance should substantially increase when we divide the applicants into groups with three or fewer reviewers and four or more reviewers. The results indicated that the proportion of variance related to applicant characteristics where the proposals had three or fewer reviewers do not differ significantly from the proportion of variance in the entire sample. They did not differ at all for the research-output measures and were only slightly higher for the "granting history" variable (years funded) and rank of current department. We may conclude that the figures presented in the tables in this section are not being significantly reduced by the possible over-representation of low-agreement cases.

We are faced with the problem of understanding the unexpectedly low correlations between characteristics of the applicants and ratings. One possible explanation would be a low level of agreement among reviewers. If, for example, an applicant with a large number of citations to past work received favorable ratings from some reviewers and unfavorable ones from others, this would yield a low or 0 correlation between citations to past work of applicants and ratings received. To what extent do the several reviewers of a given proposal agree?

To begin to estimate extent of agreement, we use the standard deviation of the reviewers' ratings. In order to estimate the amount of agreement in a given field, we computed the mean standard deviation of reviewers' ratings. The data are presented in Table 33. The mean standard deviation of reviewers' ratings varies from a low of 0.31 in algebra to a high of 0.69 in ecology and meteorology. However, in using the mean standard deviation as a measure of agreement, we must also take into account the mean rating of the reviewers. Therefore, to control for the mean rating given, we have used a coefficient of variation that is the mean standard deviation divided into the mean

TABLE 33 Consensus among Mail Reviewers: 10 Programs

Program	Mean Standard Deviation of Reviewers' Ratings	Mean of Reviewers' Ratings	Coefficient of Variation
Algebra	0.31	2.1	0.15
Anthropology	0.59	2.5	0.24
Biochemistry	0.60	2.6	0.23
Chemical Dynamics	0.42	2.3	0.18
Ecology	0.69	2.3	0.30
Economics	0.34	2.6	0.13
Fluid Mechanics	0.61	2.8	0.22
Geophysics	0.61	2.4	0.25
Meteorology	0.69	2.8	0.25
Solid-State Physics	0.35	2.2	0.16

rating. There is very little systematic variation among the 10 fields. The coefficient of variation varies from a low of 0.13 for economics to a high of 0.30 for ecology. Although these numbers are not very high, they are difficult to interpret because we do not know how much variation they represent as a proportion of the total amount of variance. We are currently using analysis of variance techniques to further investigate this important problem.

Although there might be high levels of agreement among mail reviewers, we anticipated differences in levels of agreement concerning proposals of different types of applicants. To test this assumption, we examined applicants to the biochemistry program, in which citations to recent work of applicants had a relatively high correlation with ratings received. We divided the biochemists into quintiles based upon numbers of citations to their work published between 1965 and 1974. We then compared the standard deviations separately for the bottom quintile, the top quintile, and the middle three quintiles taken together. We hypothesized that there would be more agreement on ratings for the top and bottom quintiles than for the middle group. The standard deviation for the top quintile was 0.98, the bottom quintile 1.1, and the middle group 1.1. The data clearly do not support our assumption. We must conclude that at least for applicants to the biochemistry program, there is no more agreement among reviewers of highly cited scientists than there is among the reviewers of their less-cited colleagues.

In order to eliminate the possible influence of reviewer disagreement we have computed the correlation between the mean ratings of proposals and several characteristics of the applicants. By using the mean rating (a number that has meaning only to the program director and is unknown to individual reviewers) we preclude the correlations from being lowered by disagreement. The correlations between mean ratings and individual characteristics should be substantially higher.[12] The data are presented in Table 34.

The squared correlation coefficients in Table 34 are somewhat higher than those obtained when the individual rating as opposed to the mean rating was used as the dependent variable. For example, the proportion of variance explained on ratings by log of citations to recent work for the algebra program is 0.07. The squared correlation between the mean rating received by an applicant and the log of citations to recent work for the algebra program is 0.11. We conclude, at least tentatively, that the relatively low proportions of explained variance reported in this

---

[12]This is because means cancel out random individual variation. Means almost invariably are more highly correlated (with any given variable) than individual scores.

TABLE 34 Influence of Selected Independent Variables on Mean Ratings (R^2)

Independent Variables	Algebra	Anthropology	Biochemistry	Chemical Dynamics	Ecology	Economics	Fluid Mechanics	Geophysics	Meteorology	Solid-State Physics
Log of citations to 1965-1974 work LCIT 6 (+)	0.11	0.01	0.27	0.25	0.02	0.08	0.02	0.14	0.16	0.16
Log of citations to pre-1965 work LCIT 3 (+)	0.02	0.03	0.12	0.08	0.02	0.01	0.07	0.03	0.04	0.07
Log of papers 1965-1974 LPAP 4 (+)	0.01	0.00	0.11	0.16	0.00	0.01	0.00	0.09	0.05	0.07
Years funded 1970-1974 YRSFUND (+)	0.08	0.00	0.11	0.08	0.03	0.06	0.02	0.02	0.04	0.12
Rank of present department RANKPRES (−)	0.10	0.00	0.12	0.04	0.04	0.23	0.10	0.07	0.11	0.16
Professional age DYRPHD (−)	0.01	0.00	0.01	0.01	0.00	0.00	0.00	0.00	0.01	0.06

section are not *primarily* a result of low levels of agreement among the reviewers of each proposal. It is still a question needing further research to determine exactly how much reviewer disagreement exists and the significance of such disagreement for the peer review process. This will be fully investigated and reported on in Phase 2.

The data in this section show that, on the average, reviewers' numerical ratings of proposals are not heavily influenced by the characteristics of the applicants. Perhaps they are more likely to be influenced by the reviewers' perceptions of the quality of science proposed.

Interpretations of Reviews by Program Directors

INTERPRETATIVE PROCESS

The completed review forms that come back to program directors include adjectival ratings (ranging from poor to excellent) and written comments by reviewers. Evaluation of the reviews consists not only of taking an average of the ratings but also of careful assessment of both the ratings and the comments. In other words, the program director must interpret what reviewers have presented to him.

Program directors maintain that the adjectival ratings can be evaluated only in context. Reviewers tend to develop patterns in the rating of proposals. Some use the entire rating scale; others restrict their range. Some never rate above "very good," and some never below "good." Knowledge of a reviewer's range can affect how a rating is interpreted:

We don't just look at the box that is checked. That's another thing we build up over the years, we know what people's standards are. Most of the proposals that I recommend for granting have reviews above very good. On the other hand, I have a proposal that I recommended for a grant last year that had two reviews and they both were just good. I am absolutely certain that the proposal with those two investigators was the strongest I supported. Why? I know that the people reviewing the proposal will infrequently rate a proposal higher than good.

Knowledge of a reviewer's range is useful in understanding ratings, and further interpretation is based on the written comments. Our content analysis of the reviews in the 250 jackets we examined showed that there is, in general, a strong correlation between adjectival ratings and the substantive comments. It is rare to find strongly negative substantive comments and "excellent" or "very good" adjectival ratings, or strongly positive comments and "fair" or "poor" adjectival ratings. Program directors are aware, however, that one reviewer's "excellent" may be equivalent to another's "very good."

Occasionally, there are notable discrepancies between adjectival ratings and substantive comments. One program director observed:

Frequently, people who are "soft" raters will give you a very long critical review, really pointing out what they think is wrong. Then they give you an adjective rating that is not at all commensurate with the review.

It appears that interpretation of reviews often involves considerable subtlety.

Frequently, a review is short, extremely affirmative, and rates a proposal "excellent." Some program directors maintain that this kind of review has little or no value. As one man commented:

We get reviews where somebody will say, "This is a great proposal; should be supported, excellent." That is of no use to us.

But another program director said that such reviews can be meaningful in light of the reviewer's past performance. He said:

I sent off a proposal to a _____ who is also a very good friend of mine and I got back a hastily scrawled one line comment—"I like all of these proposals." I know what he is telling me and if there were any questions asked, he would have written me a long, carefully detailed letter because he has done this in the past.

In these two cases, the reviews were "objectively" similar—both short and affirmative. However, they were responded to differently because of the program directors' knowledge of the reviewers in question.

A particularly thorny problem for program directors is evaluating negative comments by reviewers. They must determine whether such comments are based on relevant or irrelevant criteria. The following quote illustrates the difficulty:

If I get back a review that says, "On page 4, he says such and such," I have to make up my mind if he is really nitpicking because he doesn't like the man, or because he really doesn't feel this is the right way to go.

When asked how he could tell whether a negative review was a result of a personal antagonism between the applicant and reviewer, one program director responded:

It shows through by the choice of words of the reviewer. When you read it, there are tip-offs in the kinds of language a reviewer will use. They move outside of scientific language to more colorful language to describe what's wrong with the proposal.

Or, he may use his own expertise in the area in evaluating the quality of the work being proposed:

There are indications in the proposal to permit you to make judgments. There are peripheral things like a man is working in one area, but he's using a kind of instrument that I've used, an analytical instrument I'm very familiar with. This gives me a clue as to how valid the criticisms of the work are.

Or, he may call in a "neutral" third party who is knowledgeable in the area and may be able to "review the review."

If I'm not technically competent, I'll telephone someone who is neutral on the issue. You sort of divide the scientific community into two camps. There will always be fringe areas and various people that won't be in either camp, so you then try to find neutral observers to talk to.

A variation on the strategy just mentioned is contacting the applicant and asking him to respond to the criticisms that have been made. One program director described this strategy:

Very often if I am not able to come to a definitive conclusion about something on someone's review, I will call the investigator and say, "I wasn't able to understand the following question, can you help me?" Very often the man will come through with a delightfully detailed answer to the question and then follow it up with a letter. There have been times when this sort of discussion has tipped the balance in favor of a person.

These illustrations suggest that most program directors spend a great deal of time on interpretation of reviews. They view this process as a basic component of their job—as essential to a fair appraisal of the scientific merits of proposals and thus to decisions concerning them.

The interpretation and evaluation of reviews and the decision making based upon these activities are what make the activities of program directors highly demanding and professional—far beyond the routine clerking they may sometimes appear to be. This may be one reason why program directors insisted that the numerical ratings of proposals were of less use to them than were the substantive comments.

If it were possible to do the program director's job simply by computing mean scores from adjectival ratings, and to fund solely on the basis of those ratings, the position would require less scientific expertise and probably would be less attractive. One program director put it simply:

We don't only look at the box designations, we look at the actual comments. If you were merely tabulating evaluations, you wouldn't need someone with a Ph.D. to handle the job.

To interpret peer reviews intelligently and to decide whether further reviews are needed, whether a reviewer is using unfair criteria, whether one reviewer is in a better position to appraise a proposal than another, requires considerable knowledge of the social and intellectual structures of scientific fields.

TYPES OF PEER REVIEW CASES

The problems faced by program directors in decision making are best understood by examination of representative cases, which we shall now do.[1] We will present representative examples, drawn from several programs, of six different types of cases that we have identified. These are:

Unproblematic Cases:
   Reviewer agreement—positive evaluations
   Reviewer agreement—negative evaluations

---

[1] Before doing this, however, we make two general observations. The first concerns the criteria used by reviewers in evaluating applications. These differed significantly from one reviewer to another and, equally important, from one program to another. In algebra, the overwhelming majority of the comments concerned the reviewer's evaluation of the applicant's ability. In mathematics it is difficult to predict whether the applicant will actually be able to solve the problem he is proposing to work on. Reviewers' comments, therefore, are usually focused on the skill of the mathematician and the significance of the problem. But in chemical dynamics and solid-state physics, proposals are frequently to do experimental work. In these programs, reviewers are more likely to comment on the experimental design as well as the significance of the problem and the ability of the applicant. Second, reviews frequently combine two types of comments: technical substantive ones and evaluative ones. Although we did not have the time to do systematic counts of these two types of comment, it was the independent impression of all three authors that a significant majority of the reviews concentrated on evaluative statements. The majority of reviews were short, generally taking up no more than two-thirds of a page. Some, however, were several pages long. In the reviews excerpted below, we have concentrated on evaluative comments. The reader should be aware that many reviews contained detailed substantive comments.

Problematic Cases:
   Reviewer agreement on quality of "borderline cases"
   Reviewer disagreement on quality of "borderline cases"
   Weighing different decision criteria
   Apparent discrepancies between reviews and final funding decision

UNPROBLEMATIC CASES: REVIEWER AGREEMENT—POSITIVE
EVALUATIONS

Case 1

The first example is a case that was not problematical for the program director. There was complete intellectual agreement among the reviewers about the scientific merit of the proposal. The panel gave the proposal a mean rating of 1.2, and mail reviewers gave it an average rating of 1.7. (Recall that ratings range from 1 for "excellent" to 5 for "poor." In most fields, ratings tend to cluster more toward the "excellent" to "good" ratings.) After describing briefly the subject matter of the proposal, the first reviewer begins a terse evaluation:

The quality of work, the insight, and the general productivity of programs headed by _____ are, in my judgment, unsurpassed in the nation. The methodology which they have developed and the kinds of questions which their research addresses are models for the rest of the work to follow. . . . In summary, I give my highest recommendation for the continued support on this pioneering research group. (rating: 1.0)

A second reviewer of this proposal sums up his reaction with the following comments, quoted here in their entirety, except for identifying information:

I strongly recommend that this proposal be funded. The objectives of the proposal are important to both basic and applied _____. The experimental procedures have been designed with care and appear to be sound. The previous research of _____ indicates that he could conduct this research program in an excellent manner. Based upon my personal observations, I rate _____ as being possibly the most competent experimental scientist in this research area. The equipment and facilities that he has developed are excellent for the proposed research. I am a highly critical person, but I found nothing of substance to criticize in this excellent proposal. (rating: 1.0)

A third reviewer, somewhat more critical, had this evaluation:

Although I do not find the proposal to be particularly well written—particularly in terms of a sufficient explanation of experimental design and techniques to be employed, I would still strongly endorse funding of this proposal. This endorsement is based primarily upon the excellent work which has emanated from this group in the field of _____ . I have carefully followed the progress of these people over the past several years, and I am rather well convinced that some of the most incisive and yet technically advanced work in the area of _____ in the nation has been performed by this group. . . . Had this proposal come from most any other group in the country I would not provide the same enthusiastic endorsement on what is specifically contained in the proposal. (rating: 2.0)

This last reviewer is clearly emphasizing one of the NSF's stated criteria, the "track record" of the principal investigator.

The comments of the review panel are not available, but from its rating, the comments must have been strongly favorable. Even a cursory examination of the comments made by reviewers suggests that this proposal should pose few problems for a program director, unless the program has no funds to distribute.

Case 2

Another case, in the algebra program, was equally easy for the program director, although the reviewers focused more on evaluations of the abilities of particular principal investigators than on the proposal. One reviewer had this to say:

"X" and "Y" are certainly on the first team in _____ with an excellent record for producing important work. There is no doubt that they should be supported. (rating: 1.0)

The next reviewer gives specific ratings to each of the four principal investigators:

I shall treat each of the four principal investigators separately. The easiest is "X," I think. No one would question the statement that he is the best person in the field, at least until recently. Whatever he does will be important. If anyone deserves support in this area, it is he. _____ is difficult for me to judge, since I neither know him nor his work very well. He is certainly very capable, but since he publishes very little, it would perhaps be good to get an opinion on him from someone more closely involved with _____ .
_____ as I have indicated before, is in a unique position, he is extremely bright, and what he does well . . . there is no one, except perhaps _____ , who can touch him. His really brilliant work to appear in _____ on the problem of _____ is a good example of this. . . . He is very likely to produce first rate work, and should certainly be supported.

We have presented only a few out of scores of possible examples of positive evaluations that offer few problems for the program director. The forms of these evaluations vary: some concentrate on the quality of the proposed work; others on a combination of the quality of the proposal and the performance record of the principal investigators; and still others focus almost exclusively on the prior track record and prominence of the principal investigator in his field. But they all agree substantially that the grant should be made.

In sum, outstanding proposals that receive uniformly high ratings from reviewers almost invariably are funded. One program director put it this way:

There are some proposals that are very outstanding, that present new ideas, and are something that the NSF should be supporting because they have all the qualities. As a rule I would say that that sort of proposal doesn't have any difficulty—very outstanding proposals get funded no matter what!

UNPROBLEMATIC CASES: REVIEWER AGREEMENT—NEGATIVE EVALUATIONS

Case 3

In this case a proposal received uniformly negative reviews. These are selected review comments; the project was given a final rating of 3.0. The first reviewer commented:

This proposal needs quite a bit of additional work prior to funding. . . . A small sample (one man working for one-half time for 3 years) will contribute little to the store of knowledge. No science is presented or planned. With these animals it is even more imperative than in some other studies that a clear appreciation of one's scientific objectives, hypotheses be clearly stated and that experimental designs be appropriate to test those hypotheses. (rating: 3.3)

A second reviewer also is skeptical:

The objectives of the proposed study are clearly stated but the work is not put in a strong conceptual framework. The investigator proposes to do in more detail the same sorts of things that have been done elsewhere on the [animal]. Some of the primary faults of past work are not overcome because the same approach is being taken in this study. (rating: 2.8)

A third reviewer damns the proposal with faint praise:

Although this study probably will not in itself break new ground in terms of basic concepts, it should result in a solid contribution to knowledge of [animal] biology. (rating: 3.0)

In sum, there was no strong enthusiasm for this proposal from any of the reviewers, although none of them thought that it represented particularly bad science. Nonetheless, the lack of enthusiasm made it relatively easy for the program director to recommend that the request for support be declined.

Case 4

Consider a second example of clear agreement about the relatively poor quality of a proposal—this one from a social science discipline. Here are selected representative comments from the referees:

I'm not convinced that the research as now planned would be worthwhile. There has always been agreement that one should try to trace out all the costs and gains from a project. As long as the gain is judged to be worth the research cost, go ahead and fund. In this proposal, I am unenthusiastic about this prospect. (rating: 3.0)

The review just quoted was the most affirmative one received for this proposal. Another reviewer labeled the effort as a "crackpot proposal" and went on to explain why the substance of it was meaningless, rating it "poor." Another reviewer rated it "poor," saying:

I recommend that the project not be approved. Most importantly the proposal reflects no special insight concerning the three elements of the proposed study.

The final reviewer was also extremely negative. He said:

This proposal contains no evidence that the author has anything to say about this well-worn topic. There is some evidence that he does not even understand what progress has been made on these questions. (rating: 5.0)

The program director's summary reflected these reviewers' evaluations. He said:

We recommend that this disappointing proposal be turned down. The reviewers are unanimous in criticizing this proposal because of the absence of any original ideas or insights.

Two program directors summed up reactions to proposals that receive uniformly poor ratings:

There are some that are not competitive. They are dealing descriptively with phenomena and they are not addressing it in such a way that they are trying to understand and explain it. . . . It has no scientific merit.

You can read the proposal and see the sort of thing that they are doing and just know that it is just definition chasing, or generalization for the sake of generalization, and it's not exactly attacking any problems. And even if he solved the things he wanted to do, it wouldn't move [the field] forward at all. It's a weak guy and a weak problem.

PROBLEMATIC CASES: REVIEWER AGREEMENT ON QUALITY OF "BORDERLINE CASES"

In some cases there was substantial reviewer agreement that the proposals were neither excellent nor poor, and they were given relatively uniform ratings in the middle of the scale. They were judged to represent good but not outstanding science. For the program director these cases are "borderline"; they are not clearly either acceptable or rejects.

Borderline cases require that an accept-reject decision rule be applied within a restricted range of assessed quality. If program directors and panel members cannot distinguish between a set of proposals in terms of their estimated scientific worth, what criteria do they use in making decisions? This question requires further research.

Case 5

In the first borderline case we considered, there was substantial reviewer agreement that the proposal fell somewhere near the middle of the quality range—that the quality of work was likely to be mediocre. The proposal was given a summary rating of "good" by the mail reviewers and a "good" by the program director. It was declined.

One reviewer raised serious questions about the proposed methods:

The topic that ⎯⎯⎯⎯⎯⎯⎯⎯ propose to investigate is an important one. I am not that confident, however, that the proposed research methods would bear fruition in the time allowed. (rating: 3.0)

A second also raised questions about the proposed method and rated the proposal "fair" to "good." A third reviewer said the following:

The proposed research, with its emphasis on ⎯⎯⎯⎯⎯⎯⎯⎯ is a scientifically worthwhile project, and it should be attempted. I do have some questions about the proposed techniques of analysis.

He goes on to comment that the scientific competence of the investigators is sufficient to carry out the proposed research. His rating was "good."

The most critical reviewer said:

I have serious doubts concerning the contribution the proposed research will make toward improving our basic knowledge in this area. . . . Unfortunately, more than half of the author's listed references are not refereed, open-literature published articles. Furthermore, they are inaccessible to the reviewer, which makes it difficult to assess pertinent work which has been done in the past on this proposed problem. (rating: 4.0)

The program director made the following comment in his summary statement:

Very steady, if uninspired work. We just cannot afford to risk funds on a program that may be weak. The comments are excellent in scope and should be helpful to the investigator. I recommend declination.

Unlike the "clear" decline, this proposal was judged to have some merit. Had there been more resources available, it might have been funded. Also, the program director's comments imply that a resubmission responsive to reviewers' comments might be more successful the second time around.

This case is representative of many that fall near the cutting point in decisions. The principal investigator is not in competition for funds with the scientists whose proposals are given uniformly excellent reviews or with those who get uniformly poor reviews. He is competing with other principal investigators whose proposals also fall near the borderline.

Case 6

In our second borderline case, from a social science discipline, the proposal again received only intermediate ratings. Two mail reviewers rated it "good," one panel member judged it as "very good," another as "good," and another as "fair." The proposal requests somewhat more than $75,000. Here is a sampling of the reviews. One, by a panel member, gives the proposal mixed reviews:

The questions posed by [the principal investigator] are potentially quite interesting. Somehow, by the time [he] gets down to the details of his proposal, he has made them seem much less interesting. . . . In spite of my lack of enthusiasm for this proposal, I do think that [the principal investigator] does deserve some support. Much of his work shares the quality of this proposal: The topics are interesting and often reasonably original, the questions are important, the analysis is competent, and yet the whole thing is a bit prosaic. Yet his earlier work with _____ is among the best recent work in
_____ .

Another panel member was even less sure of the merits of this proposed work:

The bulk of the present proposal consists of a reprint of a paper which _____ wrote 9 months ago.

Another reviewer also expressed mixed views:

The subject is an important one. . . . The conceptual framework is straightforward, almost obvious; and accordingly, the main results obtained so far are obvious. Some important questions are overlooked. . . . Some questions are raised and answered incorrectly. . . . All in all, this would not be a bad piece of work, and he will undoubtedly get a publication out of it. I seriously question that it is worth _____ dollars.

The proposed project was funded. How was an affirmative decision made on this proposal and not on others that received roughly similar comments from peers? It appears that characteristics of the applicant might have influenced the decision, and indeed the principal investigator was an established social scientist in a major department. The program director summarizes these comments in justifying the decision:

The reviewers find that _____ is raising some interesting questions about an important problem. Most also find that the theoretical aspects of the project are the most satisfying part . . . even though they point out that there are significant omissions. . . . They foresee difficulties with the empirical testing because it is vague and not closely related to _____. [X] is an excellent _____ whose last several applications have been marginal. In this case, [A] and [B] feel he deserves support, and [C] expects he will get a publication out of the project. [D] was very supportive in the panel discussion. The program director believes that [A's] lukewarm support outweighs [E's] emphatic negative, that the project is a good one and merits approval.

Case 7

The decision in case 6 must be viewed in light of at least one other— one in which the ratings are good and the qualifications of the principal investigator are sound but in which the research proposal was declined. Here are some selected comments by reviewers in such a case:

Reviewer 1:

If [X] can deliver what he promises, it will surely be a major contribution to _____. I recommend and indeed urge support of this project.

Reviewer 2:

I am not in a position to comment on the difficulty of the proposed research. . . . I am . . . indifferent to this research.

Reviewer 3:

Another one of these narrow, highly technical proposals where some results of some use are highly likely but important results are ruled out almost a priori. . . . I would say that [X] is correct in claiming that the approaches he intends to follow are more likely to be productive than . . . [those] pursued by [Y].

Reviewer 4:

The competence and potential of the principal investigator are beyond question, and the conceptual framework of the project is sound. The chief question is whether the successful achievement of the . . . objectives of this proposed research will constitute a greater payoff to _____ , if successfully carried through.

It is difficult to see what distinguished the first borderline case that received an award from the second that was declined. Although the reviews were mixed, but generally affirmative, the program director acknowledges that he comes out feeling much as did one of the reviewers who questioned the value of the project: "But the program director ends up concurring with the judgment expressed by [reviewer 3], mainly that this is another one of these narrow, highly technical proposals where some results are almost ruled out a priori."

PROBLEMATIC CASES: REVIEWER DISAGREEMENT ON
QUALITY OF "BORDERLINE CASES"

Some cases fall near the borderline because the reviewers agree that they represent good but uninspired science. Others fall near the borderline as a result of significant reviewer disagreement, some reviewers being very affirmative and others very negative, giving the proposal a mean rating in the borderline area.

Case 8

This case involves one of the most difficult decisions faced by program directors. It produced a set of highly discrepant reviews. The mail reviews yielded an average rating of 3.0, which was high (low) enough in this program to preclude funding; the panel members gave it an average score of 2.3. The program director's final rating, however, was 1.9. Excerpts from the program director's final comments follow:

At first reading the proposal looks plausible and helpful in understanding _____ . Upon reflection it seems that the proposal also describes a lot of work that may not be useful. The implications and significance of this research are exaggerated. . . . Much of the field research conducted by this research group in the past is flawed due to faulty experimental design. We believe that this proposal is also weak in experimental design. There are too many questions on research concepts and methodology to warrant NSF support.

The project was funded. The combination of this comment by the program director and the mixed reviews by the referees called into question the final decision. We reinterviewed the program director about this case and asked for an explanation of the decision. Before looking at the program director's *post hoc* rationalizations of his decision, consider the disagreement among the referees about the merits of the proposal.

One referee's comments were essentially reproduced by the program director in his summary. This is frequently done by program directors, who go through referees' reports and extract verbatim or paraphrased sections of them for their own summaries. In this case the reviewer quoted by the program director, a panel member, gave the proposal a 4.0 ("fair") rating. But two other reviewers liked the proposal. One rated the proposal "excellent," 1.0. His one-page review, which contains little detail, says that the problem addressed is important and that the group is well equipped to conduct the research. A second affirmative review came from another program director in the same division, who rated it 2.0:

Although I am not qualified to view this proposal as an _____ expert, I did find the proposal interesting and generally understandable. I feel that the investigators are well qualified and the background and facilities for this work are excellent. . . . Overall, based on past productivity and probable future contributions from the group, I rate the proposal as good to very good.

Another panel member, in a cursory review, rated the proposal at 1.8 and supported funding. But still another reviewer rated it as "poor," 5.0, and presented a five-page, detailed, negative critique of the proposal. However, yet another reviewer rated the proposal as "very good," noting:

The research area proposed is one of the most exciting and potentially valuable areas extant to both _____ . The _____ team has been a consistent contributor to this field—some excellent, some bad; but on the whole, good to excellent.

Another reviewer thought the project was "excellent." The review, in its entirety, with deletions only for identifiable comments was:

This is a very good proposal—straightforward, workable and should contribute considerably to our knowledge of _____. [Professors A and B] have produced clean experimental results in the past and are proposing to do so in the future. As well as being good basic research, the outcome most likely will be of practical value in _____ .

Also located in the files is an instructive letter to the program director from one of the principal investigators:

I know that you are aware of the unfortunate competitive bitterness that has emerged in the field of _____. We believe it is unlikely that objective reviews can be obtained from anyone involved in the _____ program, so I am attaching a list of independent researchers who are familiar with the field and might be expected to provide fair appraisals. Perhaps you could give this some consideration. Meanwhile, we are carefully avoiding the temptation to criticize those who have attacked us, in the hope that better relations can be developed. We deeply regret the necessity to touch on this subject.

The program director is faced with a difficult decision. He has before him totally conflicting reviews, widely disparate in their appraisal of the scientific merit of the proposed research. The reviewers, who come from reputable backgrounds and many of whom are distinguished scientists in their field, disagree sharply about the qualifications of the research group proposing the research. The program director also is aware of the history of conflict within the scientific specialty. The proposal is borderline not because of agreement among referees that the proposal is of medium quality, but because of the averaging of discrepant evaluations.

We discussed the decision with the program director. Here is the exchange between us:

I: This is a grant to _____ . You had written up what seemed to be a negative summary of it. [Handed the jacket to the program director.]

S: You would be interested to know that I cited this to the guys yesterday as one of the most extremely difficult proposals that I had to decide on, and I've been here going on my seventh year. The field is so polarized, as you can see from the reviewers; they are either all good or all bad. They are either 1's or 4 or 5. In the whole field these two [principal investigators] approach the subject in a way that has antagonized many of the people. . . . They have some proponents, however, that think that they are right. So this is a very difficult thing. As I remember, I was going to decline it.

I: Yes, look at your own summary in there. That's what confused us most, otherwise we would have understood it. Your summary was taken from a review by _____ , who gave it a score of 4.0. He was a member of the panel.

S: He is our expert on these things. He is the closest thing we could come to a fairly unbiased person on this. . . . Let me tell you the whole history of this. We were all prepared to decline it and sent it down to the front office to decline it. [Mr. X], who was then deputy division director and a _____ , knew of this difficulty. _____ seemed to be dealing with this sort of thing and felt that there were too many higher ratings along with the low ratings—it was so evenly divided. [Mr. X] said if you can't get a clear reading—if some of them just "damn it to hell" and some say "good"—it's better to play it cautious than to let it go because this . . . area of _____ is one of the areas that I'm least competent in, so I would trust my own judgment less than in any other area. He said to send it to someone else. So we sent it to another batch of reviewers. We got no review from one and a 1 and a 2. So we got good readings from both of those; and on the basis of that, I proposed that we make the grant.

I: The only thing that I don't understand about it is in your summary you selected Mr. A's summary as probably the closest to your own.

S: Well, this is the place for the panel summary.

I: But that is essentially negative the way it was written. Then it was sent downstairs to _____ recommending to decline and they questioned it down there and then sent it back and you sent it out for additional reviews. Is there any indication that some external pressure was brought to bear on the Foundation to fund this proposal?

S: No, [Mr. X] felt it wasn't getting a fair shake—I felt, for gosh sakes! I've agonized with this thing for so long.

Indeed, it was clear that the program director had agonized over the decision, and it was not entirely clear to him that he had made a correct one. Later on, in discussing other problematic proposals, the same program director came squarely to the difficulty in dealing with borderline proposals:

You get advice, and if it all says the same thing, there is no problem. If either it says turn it off or turn it on, O.K. But often they don't. You get advice that's different. On the same proposal people will say it's sloppy, and others will say it's nicely put together. It's amazing when you go through this. In general, there is a certain amount of consensus. But just the ones that I've gone through lately somebody says "it's shoddily put together" and the other person says "it's the best prepared proposal I've seen in a long time." So what do I do? For my money I take my choice. So it's up to me to evaluate in part. I've read the proposal, and I've read the evaluations, and I know something about some of the guys. There are antagonisms, feuds and all sorts of things in the field.

PROBLEMATIC CASES: WEIGHING DIFFERENT DECISION CRITERIA

Case 9

In another type of problematic decision the program director must weigh different criteria of evaluation. Suppose that a proposal is considered good potential science, but the budget is very large (but necessary), or that the research facilities are poor at the applicant's institution. How does the program director handle such complications? The case that we use for illustration received strong affirmative evaluations of the competence of the principal investigator (with one notable exception), but the additional factor—the size of the budget—attracts the attention of the reviewers. The first reviewer rates the project between excellent and very good:

This is a very good application from a solid worker. The problem is interesting. They have made good progress and will continue to do so. The budget is very large and it seems to me that this should be supported by NIH. I don't think the application is so outstanding as to deserve an unusual outlay on the part of NSF, but some support should be given if needed.

A second referee, who rates it as "very good," has more reservations:

First, the investigator, Dr. X, is a very active researcher, from a good department, and has published many papers. He manages to attract good postdoctoral students and must be regarded as experienced and a well established man in his field. . . . Critique: This application is terribly verbose, disorganized and confusing to someone outside this particular area of research. Nevertheless, it is obvious that this research plan contains a lot of good ideas, and that the applicant has both the expertise and the manpower to do such experiments. On its scientific merits, this is clearly a very good application. However, I feel very strongly that Dr. X is already very generously supported. At a time when many bright young scientists cannot get funded, it seems almost unethical that others receive enormous sums. This may be understandable to top people, but Dr. X does not appear to be one of them. I would not fund this application for the reasons given above.

Finally, a third reviewer rates the project as "excellent," but voices some qualifications. One can sense some ambivalence in his comments:

_____ is a brilliant _____. He has been extremely productive in many aspects of _____ and has been, in recent years,

one of two or three leading investigators in the hot field of _____ .
We toil in the same vineyard and he scoops us three times out of four. His
record is truly excellent and promises to remain so even after he assumes some
administrative responsibilities at [University C]. There is no point in my
analyzing his research. I know it is truly outstanding. He deserves, without
question, continuing NSF support. The only real question is how much the NSF
should support his move to [University C]. Having pushed him for this and
other jobs, I feel somewhat responsible and desperately want him to succeed.
He should, and will, do a beautiful job. I also know that he is entering a
research vacuum and needs all the equipment and staff he asks for. However, I
cannot see how the NSF can afford to build up the whole show. He deserves
everything he asks for, but he simply ought to get most of it elsewhere. . . .
Therefore, my recommendation is to give him everything he wants, but since
that is impossible, I would fund him at a level higher than he gets now.

The program director's final decision was to fund, commenting: "An
excellent project from a seasoned _____ ."

The program director in this case is asked to make a decision about
the appropriate weight to give to two factors—the quality of the
proposed work and the size and type of NSF commitment to a research
program. There is little disagreement on the track record or quality of
the proposed research, but there is a general question about whether
the NSF should be in the business of building a research program for the
applying scientist at his new location. The program director in this
instance chose to ignore the monetary considerations in his summary,
although he did limit the requested funding to 1 year rather than the
requested 3 years of support.

PROBLEMATIC CASES: APPARENT DISCREPANCIES BETWEEN REVIEWS AND THE FINAL FUNDING DECISION

Let us consider even more complex cases—those in which the decision
seems to be at odds with the reviewers' evaluations. It is important to
note that the case described below is a statistical anomaly. Moreover,
it is drawn from a program in which the program director believes in
taking a far more active role in the decision-making process than do
most of the other directors that we interviewed. The case is presented
because it illustrates several important problems in the peer review
process.

Case 10

The proposal, submitted by a single principal investigator, was reviewed by four reviewers: one rated it "excellent," two "very good,"

and the fourth "good plus." Here are some selected, but entirely representative, comments by the reviewers:

Reviewer 1:

This is an excellent proposal which should lead to development of new techniques for _____. In this area Professor [B] has succeeded in providing _____. In the past, he has had remarkable success and should continue. The proposal is totally deserving of support.

Reviewer 2:

The determination of the structure of _____ is a difficult and important problem, and at present time there is little information in this area. The proposer hopes to deal with the question of the _____ and this would have many applications to _____ as well as shedding light on _____. I feel that these questions are important and that the proposer brings strong qualifications and techniques to those problems.

Reviewer 3:

The problem of funding _____ is indeed difficult. Consequently, I believe the proposal is worthwhile. In view of the proposer's past accomplishments, I believe that he is likely to accomplish his primary objectives. I do question the proposed duration of the grant.

Reviewer 4:

My only reservation about this proposal is that it is not clear why one should study _____. It is of course important to find units in _____, but I do not see any reason why units of the form stated in the proposal are useful. However, it does appear that the proposer will probably find some useful results. . . . In conclusion, I only question the value of the proposed research. However, I should add that I am not really an expert in this [specialty]. I am sure that those persons who work in a field more closely related to the proposal can give a more accurate judgment of its worth. I rate the proposal between "good" and "very good," but closer to "good."

This case is particularly interesting only because the project was declined for funding. In view of the material in the jacket, this decision seemed without explanation. While we could not understand the highly technical comments about the science, the quality evaluations were explicit and clear enough. The ratings seemed very high, and the one negative comment on the proposal was by a referee who, by his own admission, was not a specialist in the research area covered by the proposal. In a second interview with the program director, we asked him to explain his decision. Here are excerpts from the follow-up discussion with the program director:

> S: I remember that one well. We play funny games here. Once in a while you get a proposal and you are absolutely certain about how the proposal is going to turn out. I find that a lot of the problem involved in sending proposals out is knowing the reviewers and interpreting them. This is the hardest part. It's always a problem being able to calibrate the extent to which a reviewer reflects the value of a proposal. That's something of a fine-tuning process that I think just comes after a while. What I will frequently do with a proposal that I know very well is send it out to people that I have never used before. That's what I did with this one. . . . I have never before this used either _____ , _____ , or _____ [the three reviewers who gave the proposal strong, positive reviews]. This is three of the four reviewers. Reviewer "X" I knew. I know [the principal investigator] and I know his work. [Professor X], let me say in advance, on the basis of his track record, is a very, very polite gentleman who has never done anything substantial, who works on problems that are really quite routine, comes up with reasonable results. In the best of all possible worlds, or even in the very late sixties, when our funding level [was higher], we would have supported X. It's reasonable work, it's of some interest, it's the sort of thing that will be publishable, somebody will read it and grunt over it, but certainly nothing outstanding. . . . What I did with this one was send it out to four people, and I discovered of those four people, three of them were reviewers who, for one reason or another, were overly generous. So, what I'm saying is that this isn't really a fair application of the review process because in some sense I had a good idea of what the reviews were going to say in advance, or *should have said in advance*. I was using this proposal not to test the reviews of the proposal but to test the reviewers themselves. [Emphasis added.]

> I: We have some notes here of the review of [the fourth reviewer who rated the proposal between "good" and "very good"] where he says, "I should add that I'm not really an expert in _____ theory. I am sure that the persons who work in the field more closely related to the proposal can give a more accurate judgment of its worth."

> S: Excuse me for interrupting, but that's a gentlemanly way of saying that this [research area] isn't really all that interesting. [Reviewer 4] is a very, very brilliant young man, and he is right there in the middle of the mainstream of [the field] and his statement of "I am not an expert. . . ." can be interpreted as that this area of [the field] isn't really all that interesting.

If an observer from outside the scientific community—for example, a GAO auditor—examined this case without detailed knowledge of the field, it might appear to be a perfect illustration of inequity or bias—a case in which the program director disregarded the peer reviews—and it may indeed be such a case. A list of reasons that could lead a program director to decline this proposal with no sound basis for the declination could easily be developed. Here we seem to have an example of the excessive exercise of power, and this could be ammunition for the critics of the present structure of peer review. When the program director states that he knew beforehand what treatment the proposal should receive in peer reviews, he suggests that his judgment precedes the review process. Moreover, he implies that if the reviews differ from his preconception, he will alter his evaluation of the reviewers before he alters his preconception.

It may be, in fact, that this program director has for some functionally irrelevant reason declined a perfectly acceptable, even high-quality proposal. But before we can conclude that, we must consider closely some of the points made by him that may at first seem like rationalizations for a bad decision. In effect, he raises the question of weighing reviews from peers based on his own knowledge of their scientific capabilities and of their past records as reviewers. This seems like an acceptable mode of operation. Some reviewers tend to be very tough on proposals; others lenient. A casual perusal of comments, without knowledge of a reviewer's own history, could lead an outsider to incorrect inferences about the decision process. Further, some reviewers may be relatively unknown, both as scientists and as peer reviewers, while others are "world class." A terse comment by the best man or woman in a field, or one that damns a proposal with faint praise, might in fact provide a program director with more useful information than he could possibly get from five or six less-qualified reviewers. What is the program director to do, therefore, when he is faced with conflicting reviews in which the reviewer he believes to be most qualified is in a minority?

The interview excerpt quoted above also presents other problems. In his *post hoc* interpretation, the program director tells us that he can read between the lines of reviewer 4, that he can tell that the reviewer is actually quite negative about the substance of the proposal, that the reviewer really is unenthusiastic about it, and that the reviewer believes that it should be declined. Clearly, on the surface this position is not very convincing, and it may be that even below the surface, the reviewer was not trying to communicate a negative evaluation to the program director. In some cases—particularly in those involving a long-standing relationship between the reviewer and the program director—subtle judgments can be conveyed through the use of language. Most scientists who serve on review panels, or who have had occasion to read many referee reports for journal articles, are fully aware that there are code words and modes of negative judgments in such reports.

The program director says he uses certain proposals not only for evaluating the scientific merits of their content but also as a device for evaluating new reviewers. The initiation of new reviewers into the peer review system is not done systematically at the NSF.

Finally, this example underscores how difficult it is in the end to demonstrate conclusively that particularistic criteria have influenced a specific decision. To be sure, this case represents a statistical anomaly, but even here it is difficult indeed to "prove" that an unfair judgment has been reached or, correlatively, to "disprove" the claim that it was a fair judgment.

A PARADOX ABOUT INFLUENCES ON REVIEWER RATINGS

Even the casual reader of this report must have noticed an apparent inconsistency in the data reported. On the one hand, the quantitative data on the influences on ratings suggest that the personal and social characteristics of principal investigators do not affect in a major way the evaluations of quality by peers. On the other hand, we have presented qualitative data—drawn from interviews with program directors and panel members as well as from NSF proposal jackets—that suggest that the track records of particular principal investigators explicitly enter the peer evaluations and have an important effect on funding decisions. How is it possible to find frequent references to the track records, eminence, and social statuses of scientists in actual reviewer comments and yet find low correlations between these same variables and proposal ratings?

This apparent discrepancy might be explained in several ways. One explanation is that referees first read and evaluate the contents of scientific proposals on their merits. They decide whether they should be funded or not and then construct arguments to support their decisions and justify their ratings. They comment on the technical science and then, because of explicit instructions from the NSF, they refer to the track records of the principal investigators and their ability to carry out the proposed research. This explanation assumes that the basic adjectival evaluations are made on the contents; the proposals are given tentative ratings; and then the qualitative comments are constructed to conform to NSF criteria and to justify the evaluations of the proposals. In justifying ratings it is certainly easier and less time consuming to make evaluative comments on applicants' qualifications than to make substantive comments on the contents of proposals.

At first this explanation seems almost naive, because we can instantly think of cases in which the evaluation was influenced by knowledge about principal investigators. The first two things that most reviewers look at are the titles and names of the principal investigators. As soon as the name is observed, a set of "evaluations" has already been made. But this may be true only for a very small fraction of the population in a field—those who are widely known.[2]

Each of us can think of a few scientists to whom we would give excellent ratings even if their proposals were disappointing. In some such instances, reviewers may actually doubt their ability to understand correctly the contents of the proposals. As one program director said:

There are certain [scientists] who have been doing such good work for a while that unless something drastic happens to them mentally, you know that as long as there is federal support in [the field], these guys should get support.

These few scientists notwithstanding, it seems plausible that the ratings of proposals and the evaluations of the characteristics of principal investigators could be quite independent of each other. Further, even if a reviewer knows an applicant's work, in most cases he can keep that knowledge from influencing his evaluation of a current proposal. We would conjecture that only in a small number of cases does the high quality of past performance override the judgment that a proposal is weaker than expected.

Another explanation for the seeming discrepancy between the quantitative and qualitative data relates to self-selection of applicants for NSF grants. It is possible that a substantial majority of applicants have good track records and that differentiation among them is usually based upon the perceived quality of the proposal. Clearly, one possible reason for the low correlation between ratings and applicant characteristics is that most applicants to the NSF are already among the top scientists in their fields. Thus, if many scientists are going to be denied funding, a good share of them are apt to have substantial track records

---

[2]Data from an unpublished study (Cole, 1971) indicate that random samples of scientists located at ACE-ranked institutions generally have low visibility to their colleagues. The average scientist's name is known to only approximately 30 percent of the people working at these same ACE-ranked institutions.

or to be located at major centers of scientific activities. The presence of substantial numbers of relatively eminent scientists among those denied funding, of course, reduces the association between ratings and the characteristics of the applicants. At this point we have only limited and fragmentary data on the extent to which NSF applicants differ in eminence from a random sample of scientists in their fields.

Influence on Decision

Thus far, in tracing the course of a proposal from the time that it is submitted until a decision is made, we have investigated the ways in which reviewers are selected, the possible interactions between reviewers and applicant characteristics, and the influence of principal investigators' characteristics on ratings given by peer reviewers. After the peer reviewer makes his evaluation of the proposal, he sends his rating back to the program director. When the program director has received the reports of mail reviewers and when the panel (for those programs with panels) has met, the program director must make a decision to fund or not to fund. In the previous section, we discussed the ways in which the program director interprets reviews of proposals.

We would expect that the ratings given proposals by peer reviewers (both *ad hoc* mail reviewers and panels) should be the most important influence on program directors' decisions. We also would expect that program directors would exercise some discretion in making grants and that there would not be perfect correlations between ratings given by peer reviewers and funding decisions. In this section we attempt to estimate the effect of peer ratings and some of the characteristics of applicants on funding decisions.

Identifying the factors affecting the granting decisions presents a difficult methodological program—how to deal with a dichotomous dependent variable. Although conceptually the proposals could be ranked from the "most meritorious" to the "least meritorious," in fact they must be divided into two groups: those to be funded and those to be denied funding. To deal with this problem, we exhibit and analyze tables as well as use special analytic techniques that rely upon additional assumptions. Each method has advantages and disadvantages. For the purpose of assessing the effect of one independent variable when the others are fixed, the most satisfactory approach is probably that based on contingency tables, which does not require the assumptions of normality and linearity. However, for each of the 10 programs we have approximately 120 cases, too few for an analysis of this type to yield a reasonably precise quantitative measure of the effect of one variable when the others are fixed. Therefore, we decided to use correlation and multiple regression techniques. The particular form we use is probit analysis, which was developed by biologists studying drug dosage levels and which has been used extensively by economists and political scientists for analyzing data involving dichotomous dependent variables. (See Appendix B for a discussion of this method.) These techniques assume that the probability of funding is a normal distribution function evaluated at a linear function of the independent variables. We do not have enough data to test whether these assumptions are valid throughout the study. In fact, some of the tables show that the linearity assumption does not hold. In these cases the tables give more information than probit (see Table 54, for example, and the discussion concerning it on pages 145-147).

We are aware of the deficiencies of probit analysis described above, and also of the desirability of discovering a reasonably accurate structural model rather than simply imposing a model (probit) from which to infer the degree of effect of certain variables. Nevertheless, we have chosen this statistical tool for two reasons: (1) It is standard methodology for social science that yields a measure of association R^2, which is at least qualitatively meaningful, even if the assumptions are not satisfied exactly. (2) When we compare qualitative results inferred from the tabular data with the probit results and with the standard regression analysis (which also assumes linearity) we have found almost complete agreement.

Table 35 presents the proportions of variance in decisions explained by the mean ratings given proposals by mail reviewers and the proportions of variance explained by the mean ratings given by panels (for programs that use panels). The last column of Table 35 shows the total amounts of variance in decisions explained by both the ratings given by mail reviewers and the ratings given by panel members. (These are estimates from probit multiple regression equations.) With two exceptions, the ratings given by peer reviewers (both the *ad hoc* mail reviews and the panel reviews) explain the bulk of the variance in decisions

TABLE 35 Probit Estimated R^2 for Rating of Reviewers (and Panels Where They Exist): 10 Programs

	Dependent Variable = Decision		
	1	2	3
Program	Mean Rating Given by Mail Reviewers	Mean Rating Given by Panel	Total (Mail + Panel)
Algebra	0.76	–	0.76
Anthropology	0.63	0.52	0.83
Biochemistry	0.74	0.52	0.86
Chemical Dynamics	0.92	–	0.92
Ecology	0.44	0.70	0.77
Economics	0.50	0.56	0.78
Fluid Mechanics	0.57	–	0.57
Geophysics	0.49	–[a]	0.49
Meteorology	0.92	–	0.92
Solid-State Physics	0.70	–	0.70

[a]Panel ratings for this program were unavailable.

made. In fact, in two of the programs, chemical dynamics and meteorology, almost all the variance in decisions is explained by the ratings given by mail reviewers.

The two programs in which less variance in decisions is explained by ratings are geophysics and fluid mechanics. The geophysics program uses both *ad hoc* mail review and a panel. Unfortunately, however, no data are kept on panel meetings or the ratings given by panel members. Thus, the ratings and the influence that they presumably exerted on the program director cannot be included in this quantitative analysis. However, if we compare geophysics with other programs that use panels, we can estimate that if we had the data on the panel ratings, the total amount of variance explained by the peer review evaluations would be significantly greater for geophysics. The mail review ratings alone explain 49 percent of the variance in that program. This is comparable to the amount explained by the mail ratings in other programs using panels. For example, in economics, 50 percent of the variance was explained by mail review ratings alone, and in ecology, 44 percent was explained by mail review ratings alone. In biochemistry and anthropology, slightly more variance was explained by the mail reviews alone. If geophysics were run the same as, let us say, ecology and economics, we can presume that the total amount of variance explained by both panel ratings and mail review ratings would be approximately 75 percent. Without data on the panel ratings this must remain a plausible speculation.

The reason for the relatively small amount of variance explained in decisions by peer review ratings in the fluid mechanics program is difficult to determine. It is possibly a result of the management style of the program director. It is possible for a program director to make decisions that do not completely correspond with the mean ratings of proposals. It is also possible that the fluid mechanics program director did not depend as much upon the adjectival ratings as upon the verbal comments made by the peer reviewers and that the correlation between the adjectival ratings and the substance of the comments was less in this program than in others. Nonetheless, a substantial amount of variance in decisions is explained in fluid mechanics, the program that we believe shows the least influence of the peer reviewer ratings.

The general conclusion to be drawn from Table 35 is that the crucial variable in determining whether or not a grant is made is the mean of the adjectival ratings given by the mail reviewers and the panel reviewers. This seems to contradict the accounts of the program directors that we reported in the previous section. Most of the program directors told us that they paid more attention to the substantive comments than to the numerical or adjectival ratings. There are several plausible explanations for this seeming contradiction.

1. The program directors may have exaggerated the necessity of being able to interpret the substantive comments in order to enhance the importance of their role.

2. As noted above, there is a high degree of correspondence between the substantive comments and the numerical ratings. Therefore, we would expect to find a high correlation between mean ratings and decisions even if the program directors were, in fact, basing their decisions primarily on the substantive comments.

3. It is in the problematic cases, in which the program director's decision is difficult, that careful examination of the substantive comments is the most important. These difficult cases take up most of the program director's time and therefore stand out in his view. Thus, the program directors may have been more likely to report their procedures on these cases than on the numerically more frequent ones that were less problematic.

4. The correlation between peer review ratings and decisions was not perfect. This may reflect the lack of perfect correspondence between the substantive comments and the numerical ratings. For cases in which the two parts of the peer review evaluation do not correspond, the program director may be giving greater weight to the substantive comments than to the numerical ratings.

Thus, upon closer inspection, we tentatively conclude that there is probably no contradiction between the accounts of the program directors and the data reported in Table 35.

ACCUMULATIVE ADVANTAGE

Although the ratings given by the peer reviewers are clearly the most significant influence on program directors' decisions, the correlation between these ratings and decisions, as we have said, is not perfect. We wanted to observe the extent to which the program director was influenced by some of the personal characteristics of applicants.

Past work in the sociology of science has led us to expect that eminent scientists would be at an advantage in the competition for NSF funds. A social process called "accumulative advantage" (Merton, 1942; Cole and Cole, 1973; Allison and Stewart, 1974; Zuckerman, 1977) is related to this expectation. In this process, people who have been rewarded at time 1 have a better chance of being rewarded at time 2, *independent of the quality of their role performance* at time 2.

We have enough data to make a rough test of the extent to which accumulative advantage operates in the NSF peer review process. Except for the effect of past funding history, the data show little evidence that it significantly affects the funding of proposals by the NSF. Since, however, there is a growing literature in the sociology of science developing this concept, it is important that we explain its meaning and expand on our findings. The idea is a simple one: it is predicated upon the notion that young scientists who are most talented and who have opportunities for obtaining resources and facilities can, in fact, make use of those resources and facilities to become more productive scientists than others within their age cohort who do not have the same access to resources and facilities.

Critics of the peer review process as it currently operates assert in so many words that accumulative advantage, not based upon demonstrated ability, operates in a self-reinforcing way to exclude able scientists from the funds needed for research. An "in group" of scientists, predominantly located at the most prestigious and powerful universities, becomes established, whose members give funds to their own colleagues, thereby enabling them to publish more scientific papers and to lay claim to future resources on the basis of their established track records.

Few scientists would argue that past performance should not count in evaluating potential to make scientific discoveries. But how much do track record and other indications of status count in the peer review process, and what evidence exists to substantiate or repudiate claims that accumulative advantage operates to reward some scientists at the expense of others equally qualified? These questions were raised in our interviews with program directors.

Program directors differ on how much weight should be given to track records in evaluating proposals. Some believe the track record is most important:

I think that track record counts very heavily. I would rather fund a somewhat average proposal from an outstanding investigator than I would fund an outstanding proposal from an average investigator, simply because it's not so difficult to sit down and say, "This is an obvious problem; it should be solved." Everyone can pick out important problems, but not everyone can solve them. This has to be taken into account very heavily.

On the other hand, some reviewers and program directors believe that funding decisions should be based solely on the merits of current proposals. One program director articulated this position:

We put a lot of emphasis on the document. Sometimes they are not as good as they should be. We faced this issue specifically in one area where some obviously competent people turned in proposals that said, "Send me money, I'm so and so." If we say, "All right, we know what he's doing; we ought to give him some money," it would be unfair to young investigators. So we have decided to take a deliberate stance and go with the document. It's got to be a good document, and if it's a famous investigator, then he better "pull his socks up."

Critics of peer review have expressed the extreme view that it is virtually impossible for eminent scientists to have proposals rejected, regardless of their quality. We talked to people at the Foundation about the treatment of eminent scientists. Dealing with proposals from eminent scientists occasionally does present problems for program directors. When the proposals from eminent scientists are imaginative and well prepared, they present few problems. Problems arise for program directors, however, when an eminent scientist submits a proposal perceived by the reviewers as being of lower than expected quality.

Most program directors believe that a relatively poor proposal from an eminent person generally means one of two things: (1) the person has peaked and is no longer doing high-quality work or (2) the person has not taken the time to write a good proposal because he has the attitude that if he asks for money, he should "automatically" get it. As one program director put it:

If we get a lousy proposal from an eminent person, we have to decide whether he is on his last legs or whether he made an assumption that everybody knew what he could do.

The assessment that an investigator is no longer capable of doing such good work is a difficult one to make, of course. This is largely dependent on the program director's ability to get an evaluation of the investigator's most recent work. As one person said:

When one of these people gets reviews that say, "All this person has done is dick around with definitions for the last 3 years," it won't go.

Another program director spoke of the difficulty in making such a judgment about a prominent scientist. He said:

This is tremendously difficult. Here is somebody that's really done something outstanding in the past, he's set up a whole subfield of science, and we're sitting here playing God, saying that his research productivity is coming to an end.

In cases in which the prevailing opinion is that the principal investigator has not taken the time to write a good proposal, different positions are taken by program directors. Some report that they are apt to give a person the benefit of the doubt and fund the proposal.

A variation on this position is to fund, but at a lower level than requested. A program director described this in the following way:

I got a so-so proposal from an "eminent." Since he was eminent and I would expect him to continue to do good work, I telephoned him and told him exactly what was going on. I told him, I'm not going to put $50,000 into this, but I will give you $20,000 with the expectation that good science would be done and that a better renewal would come in.

There are other ways in which reduced funding is employed in these cases. Some program directors give people terminal support, hoping that this will be taken as a threat and "light a fire" under the investigator and that he will resume working at the level he had worked at in the past.

Other program directors handled this discrepancy by declining to support the principal investigator but strongly suggesting that the proposal be resubmitted in a better, more complete form:

If they're still productive and through complacency just wrote a thin proposal, we won't banish them to Siberia. We'll say, "Give us some more details; what is it you're really up to?" And they'll probably make it.

There are those, though, who take a harder line and decline proposals from "eminents" with no implicit or explicit promise of another look. Some are just put off by the attitude that all one needs to do is submit a blank check because one is eminent. A program director described such a case:

There was one principal investigator who said he was too busy to take the time to write a good proposal. He got turned down. He said, "Do you mean to tell me that if Newton came to you, you would refuse him?" I told him, "Unfortunately, we do not deal with Newtons in our daily lives here."

Another said:

There were a number of cases where we received proposals from eminent people in the field and the proposal was three pages. It said something like, "I'm me, give me the money." There was no way that person was going to get something out of me or the panel. We were insulted.

What can we conclude from these qualitative interviews about the effect of accumulative advantage on peer review decisions? In general, program directors testify that the major factor in decisions is the comments and ratings given to proposals by mail reviewers and panel members. To the extent that these reviewers include in their evaluations comments about the track records or prior performance of principal investigators, such factors may enter into the decision-making process. But few program directors suggested that the status of a scientist in the social-stratification system of science was a major factor in their decisions. They asserted, with a number of exceptions, that their decisions were, for the most part, not particularly influenced by knowledge of the scientist's academic affiliation, his rank, prior history of funding, and the like.

Questions about sex and race bias only elicited the response that few women and minority group members applied for funds, and that, when they did, these functionally irrelevant statuses had no influence on decisions. Program directors tended to stress a particular concern with younger scientists beginning their careers. Special efforts were made to get people going on research, not to "turn them off" if they had any potential—indeed, to favor the young in cases in which their proposals were similar in quality to those of older scientists.

But these assertions and comments by program directors are, we would expect, somewhat normative responses. We cannot expect program directors, section heads, and other NSF officials to state openly that they favor one type of scientist over another when they cannot distinguish them by the quality of their proposals. Actually, some were very candid about the difficulty in arriving at decisions in closely competitive situations. To ascertain the extent to which the characteristics of applicants influence program directors' decisions we turn to an analysis of the 1,200 applicants in 10 programs.

INFLUENCE OF PAST RESEARCH OUTPUT

To what extent do eminent investigators actually have a better chance of receiving grants, independent of the reviewer ratings of their proposals? We have no direct measure of "eminence." Citations to past work and numbers of papers published, however, are good indirect indicators of scientists' positions in the social-stratification system of science.

In order to analyze the relationship between scientific output as measured by citations and number of papers published and granting decision separately for each program, we shall use probit analysis.[1] The results are presented in Table 36. To be perfectly clear about the content of Table 36, note that it contains six probit regression equations for each field. The first three probit equations presented in columns 1, 2, and 3 represent two-variable relationships, one independent and one dependent variable. The data presented in column 4 represent probits involving three independent variables, that is, the three productivity measures: citations to recent work, citations to old work, and number of papers published in the last 10 years. Column 5 presents a probit regression that includes only the mean rating and the panel ratings. Column 6 contains probit regressions that include five independent variables: the mean rating; the panel rating; and the three productivity measures above. Column 7 simply represents the differences in the estimated R^2 that are obtained by subtracting the figures in column 5 from those in column 6.

The first three columns of Table 36 show the amounts of variance in each of the 10 programs accounted for by each of the three research-productivity measures separately. The data in these three columns are less significant for what they tell us about the influence on program directors' decisions than they are concerning the types of scientists who are more or less likely to receive NSF grants. We would have the same expectations for these data that we had when we analyzed the influence on reviewer ratings. We would expect that scientists who had done the most important work in the past, as measured by the numbers

---

[1]See the caveat at the beginning of this section.

TABLE 36 Influence of Productivity Measures on Decision (Probit Estimated R^2)

Program	1 Citations to Work between 1965-1974	2 Citations to Work before 1965	3 Publications between 1965-1974	4 Three Productivity Measures	5 Mean Rating Plus Panel Rating	6 Mean Rating, Panel Rating, Plus Three Productivity Measures	7 Difference
Algebra	0.08	0.04	0.00	0.14	0.76	0.82	0.06
Anthropology	0.03	0.02	0.00	0.04	0.83	0.86	0.03
Biochemistry	0.37	0.10	0.18	0.38	0.86	0.86	0.00
Chemical Dynamics	0.31	0.10	0.24	0.32	0.92	0.93	0.01
Ecology	0.20	0.07	0.03	0.22	0.77	0.80	0.03
Economics	0.19	0.03	—[a]	0.26[a]	0.78	0.78[a]	0.03
Fluid Mechanics	0.08	0.20	0.05	0.21	0.57	0.66	0.09
Geophysics	0.15	0.08	0.20	0.21	0.49	0.59	0.10
Meteorology	0.12	0.01	0.05	0.13	0.92	0.93	0.01
Solid-State Physics	0.24	0.18	0.13	0.32	0.70	0.77	0.07

[a]For this field, publications was excluded, since it had a slight negative association with the dependent variable.

of their publications and citations of them, would be more likely to receive NSF grants than those whose work had been judged to be less important. The data in column 1 of Table 36 indicate great variation in the extent to which citations to recent work (work published between 1965 and 1974) are correlated with decisions. The estimated R^2 goes from a low of 0.03 for anthropology to a high of 0.37 for biochemistry. However, in five of the fields—biochemistry, chemical dynamics, ecology, economics, and solid-state physics—this variable has at least a moderate correlation with decisions.[2] There is also a moderate correlation between citations to recent work and decisions in geophysics and meteorology. In fluid mechanics and algebra the correlations are lower.

What can we conclude from these data? Although the strength of the correlation varies significantly among the 10 programs, in most of the programs, scientists who have done work often cited in the past are considerably more likely to receive grants from the NSF. The correlation, however, is far from perfect. This indicates that the grant proposals of some scientists who are often cited are being turned down, while at the same time, the proposals of other scientists, with fewer citations, are being approved.

These findings suggest several interesting questions. Why are the proposals of scientists whose recent work is very highly cited turned down? Are these scientists becoming less productive (a fact known to reviewers although not evident from the longer-term citation index) or do they continue to do important work but do not write detailed, good proposals? Also, why are scientists funded whose work has not been cited at all? Are these predominantly young scientists without track records, or are grants being given to some established scientists whose work has not been widely used by the scientific community? We searched for answers to these questions, looking in depth at the "deviant" cases in 3 of the 10 fields: chemical dynamics, biochemistry, and solid-state physics. Deviant cases are here defined as scientists in the highest citation quintile who are *not* funded and scientists in the lowest citation quintile who *are* funded. We pulled the jackets on all these cases in three programs (biochemistry, chemical dynamics, and solid-state physics), and considering the vitae of the scientists, reviewers' comments, and comments of program directors, we assessed the reasons for funding decisions.

The general conclusion of this analysis was that the decision-making procedure followed by the NSF is, indeed, open. The proposals of some

[2]By social science standards, some of these correlations would be considered large.

quite eminent scientists have been turned down, and many young and relatively unestablished scientists are funded.

There was no evidence for the conclusion that the highly cited scientists who are not funded are "over the hill." All highly cited scientists who were not funded show evidence of continuing to be highly productive. Proposals of highly cited scientists are turned down for several reasons. In some cases the proposals are very weak and receive unfavorable evaluations. For example, a declined proposal in chemical dynamics had two principal investigators, one listing 75 publications and the other 45. The reviewers were virtually unanimous in their conclusion that the proposal contained too little detail and that it was impossible to assess the merits of what would be done on the basis of the proposal. The program director concluded: "The work proposed here is not adequately described. Details of indication of importance are missing." One reviewer commented: "It [the proposal] was written in a casual, almost half-hearted way." Thus, the proposals of experienced, highly published chemists can be turned down if the reviewers agree that they give no indication of important work that will be done with the grant funds.

In other cases, eminent investigators are turned down because they already have other sources of funding. These may be other NSF funds or funds from other agencies. For example, one eminent principal investigator who was turned down in the chemical dynamics program reports that he concurrently held a large grant in the NSF RANN program.[3] Another applicant to the chemical dynamics program, a member of the National Academy of Sciences, who was turned down, concurrently held an NSF basic research grant in another chemistry program. He also concurrently held a grant from the Petroleum Research Fund of the American Chemical Society. A rejected applicant in the biochemistry program reports that he is currently funded by the NIH with a $50,000 grant and has applied for an additional $100,000 from the NIH. In solid-state physics a rejected eminent applicant reports holding a $22,000 grant in another NSF program and additional support from the Air Force.

[3]The unit of analysis for this study has been the individual applicant to the NSF. We have no data, nor does the NSF to our knowledge have data, on whether or not applicants to the NSF have received grants from other agencies in the past. Although eminent scientists may have an only slightly higher probability of receiving a grant from the NSF on a particular application, their overall probability of being funded either by the NSF or in general may be considerably higher. This could happen if they made multiple applications to the NSF and/or other funding agencies. Further research is needed on the varying probabilities of different types of scientists receiving funding from any source.

In some cases that we examined, we found that rejected proposals from eminent investigators had not received uniformly bad reviews but either mixed or good reviews. Also there was no evidence that the principal investigator had funds from another source. It is possible, of course, that in some cases decisions can be explained as mistakes of program directors.

Some applicants have received NSF grants who had either zero or very few citations to work published within the past 10 years. Some of these had published many articles but had not often been cited. As has frequently been pointed out, number of citations is only a rough indicator of the quality of work and should not be considered a decisive indicator in particular cases. Some scientists who have made significant contributions are not frequently cited, and others whose contributions are of less importance have been frequently cited. Thus, the finding that some scientists who appear to be ranked low in the stratification system (as indicated by the number of citations to their recent work) may in part be explained as a result of measurement error. In other cases we found examples of scientists who were relatively young and had little track record who submitted proposals that were highly rated and funded.

Returning to the question with which we began the analysis of the influence of past scientific productivity on NSF decision making, to what extent does past research productivity influence decisions independent of the ratings received? Since the ratings given by peer reviewers are so clearly the most important determinant of decisions, analysis of the influence of any of the principal investigators' characteristics studied in this report on the decisions made required determining how much variance was explained by those characteristics after controlling, so to speak, for the mean ratings of reviewers and panels.

Column 4 of Table 36 presents the estimated proportion of variance in decisions explained by combination of the three research-output measures (citations to recent work, citations to old work, and number of recently published papers).[4] Column 5 gives the estimated proportion of variance explained by reviewer ratings. (These are the same figures that appeared in column 3 of Table 35.) Column 6 shows the total amount of variance in decisions explained by the three research-output variables and the reviewer ratings.

Subtracting the number in column 5 from that in column 6, we obtain

---

[4]Note that in some fields (biochemistry and chemical dynamics) there is a good deal of multicolinearity among the three output measures. Also note that in algebra the three variables together explain more variance than the sum of the amount explained separately. This is not unusual or indicative of error in probit equations.

an estimate of the influence of past research output on decisions, independent of reviewer ratings.[5] This figure varies from a low of 0.00 for biochemistry to a high of 0.10 for geophysics.[6] It is important to note that we are aware that all the covariance between ratings and past productivity is being assigned to the ratings. For many substantive problems such a stepwise procedure would be misleading, but here we are interested essentially in how much weight in decision making the program director gives to status characteristics beyond those status elements that are "built into" the rating system. In general, we conclude that there is very little evidence that scientists whose past work has been frequently cited and who have published many papers benefit more than slightly from accumulative advantage. Given equal proposal ratings, highly published and cited scientists are not much more likely than those with fewer papers and citations to receive NSF grants. Since we have already shown in section 3 that the ratings are not heavily influenced by applicant characteristics, we can tentatively conclude that accumulative advantage does not play a significant role in the 10 programs we have studied.

Given the very high correlations of mean ratings by reviewers and panels with decisions, it is not surprising that past research performance would add only a small amount to the explained variance.[7] Program directors are using peer reviews to make their decisions in those cases in which reviews clearly differentiate among proposals.

[5]To be statistically more precise, we have an estimate of the proportion of variance explained by the research-output measures not already explained by reviewer ratings.
[6]Recall that we do not have panel data for geophysics, the addition of which could reduce this figure. Although one could list (for example) the amount of variation explained by ratings not already accounted for by citation index, we have chosen in column 7 to emphasize the amount of variation already explained by the reviewer rating. This is because we are primarily interested in how much weight in decision making the program director gives to status characteristics above and beyond those status elements that are "built into" the rating system.

The reader will also note that here as in section 3 we present R^2 statistics rather than regression coefficients that are part of the structural models. We do this for two reasons: the first is the substantive point made above, and the second is the difficulty in determining the relative weights to be given to various independent variables.
[7]Because the peer ratings explain so much variance there is not much left to be explained by other variables. However, even if we examine the proportion of remaining variance (after ratings have been entered in the equation) explained by the output measures, we find no program in which these variables explain more than 25 percent of the remaining variance.

GRANTING HISTORY

We now study how past funding by the NSF influences current funding decisions. Table 37 shows the proportion of applicants in each program who have not applied for NSF funds within the previous 5 years. In 7 of the 10 programs, 70 percent or more of the sample of applicants have applied for NSF funds between 1970 and 1974. Most of the nonapplicants probably have never applied for NSF funds. The proportion of first-time applicants in algebra, anthropology, and economics is significantly higher than in the other programs. This is probably because these 3 programs have been growing rapidly in the last 5 years.

We also have data on the number of years between 1970 and 1974 in which applicants have received NSF funds. The notion of accumulative advantage would lead us to expect that past grant recipients would have an advantage over nongrant recipients independently of the ratings their proposals received.

Most program directors claimed that the granting history of applicants had little effect on current decisions. Some said that the NSF records of granting history were in such disarray that it was difficult for program directors to obtain such information if they wanted it. Perhaps the program directors were answering normatively, but most claimed that whether or not an applicant was a recent or current grant recipient had little independent effect on decisions. They also pointed out that there was, in general, a fairly high correlation between the quality of past work supported by NSF grants and the quality of current proposals.

TABLE 37 Applicants Not Having Applied for
NSF Funds between 1970 and 1974

Program	Percent Not Applying
Algebra	37
Anthropology	48
Biochemistry	30
Chemical Dynamics	24
Ecology	30
Economics	54
Fluid Mechanics	28
Geophysics	23
Meteorology	25
Solid-State Physics	27

Some programs are more concerned with funding history than others. These differences tend to be related to the structure of the scientific discipline. Some projects in physics, for instance, are not really conceived as projects of limited duration, even if program directors receive new proposals every few years from the principal investigators or heads of laboratories. When the NSF invests large sums of money in physical hardware required for specific lines of scientific inquiry, they often think of the investment in relation to a 6- to 10-year period—or longer. Grants that are made with this expectation are carefully reviewed by site visitors and program directors, but given available funds, there is an expected continuity of funding. In such cases, granting history clearly influences the probability of further support. One program director in physics put it this way:

Clearly, if you go into something like that (an $8,000,000 to $17,000,000 investment in equipment), you don't casually drop out of it. You are more likely to go in and say, "Look, we've got to beef this program up a little, but with new people, better people, so that we can really get this instrument to perform according to its capabilities."

The data on granting history are presented in Table 38. The data in the first column show that in most of the programs (with the exception of anthropology) past grant recipients do have a higher probability of receiving grants than do those who have received little or

TABLE 38 Influence of Granting History on Decision
(Probit Estimated R^2)

Program	Dependent Variable = Decision			
	1 Years Funded, 1970-1974	2 Mean Rating Plus Panel Rating	3 Mean Rating, Panel Rating, Plus Years Funded	4 Difference
Algebra	0.12	0.76	0.76	0.00
Anthropology	0.01	0.83	0.85	0.02
Biochemistry	0.19	0.86	0.86	0.00
Chemical Dynamics	0.14	0.91	0.92	0.01
Ecology	0.17	0.77	0.78	0.01
Economics	0.08	0.78	0.78	0.00
Fluid Mechanics	0.15	0.57	0.64	0.07
Geophysics	0.16	0.49	0.56	0.07
Meteorology	0.07	0.92	0.92	0.00
Solid-State Physics	0.38	0.70	0.77	0.07

TABLE 39 Effect of Mean Rating of Reviewers and Granting History
on Decision: Two Fields

Mean Rating of Reviewers	Solid-State Physics, % Receiving Grants					
	Former Grant Recipients		Former Nonrecipients		Totals	
2.00 or less	100	(37)	82	(28)	92	(65)
2.01 or more	50	(12)	5	(44)	14	(56)
TOTAL	88	(49)	35	(77)		

Mean Rating of Reviewers	Geophysics, % Receiving Grants					
	Former Grant Recipients		Former Nonrecipients		Totals	
2.00 or less	100	(27)	79	(14)	93	(41)
2.01 or more	57	(37)	28	(32)	43	(69)
TOTAL	75	(64)	44	(46)		

no support from NSF in the past 5 years. This is notably true in
solid-state physics.

An especially significant question is the extent to which past grant
recipients have an advantage over nonrecipients of grants when their
proposals receive roughly the same ratings. As the figures in the last
column of Table 38 indicate, accumulative advantage has an effect in 3
of the 10 programs: fluid mechanics, geophysics, and solid-state
physics.[8] In these three disciplines, among proposals receiving about
the same peer review ratings, the program directors are more likely to
make awards to current or recent grant recipients than to scientists
who have received little or no NSF support in the past.

To illustrate the effect of this factor in two of the programs, we
present the data in Table 39. In Table 38 we showed that granting
history had an independent effect on decisions in solid-state physics. In
Table 39, we use tabular analysis to show the independent effect of
granting history on decisions when controlling for mean ratings by
reviewers. We point out that in general, the mean ratings of reviewers
determine whether or not grants are given. Ninety-two percent of
applicants receiving mean scores of 2.0 or lower (a low number is a

[8]It is necessary to point out again that the finding in geophysics could be a result of not
including the panel ratings.

high rating) received grants. Only 8 percent of those receiving such low scores did not receive grants. And only 14 percent of those who received scores above 2.0 received grants. We also point out that 88 percent of past grant recipients received grants, as compared with only 35 percent of nonrecipients. Moreover, the former grant recipients were considerably more likely to receive high mean scores than were the nonrecipients. About three-fourths of the former grant recipients received mean scores of 2.0 or lower, whereas only slightly more than a third of the nonrecipients received scores of 2.0 or lower.

Among applicants who received mean scores of 2.0 or less, 100 percent of former grant recipients received current grants. Among those who had not received NSF grants before but who received essentially the same scores on their current applications, 82 percent received grants. Even more interesting is what happened to applicants who got poorer scores, those higher than 2.0. Among those, fully 50 percent who were former grant recipients received current grants, whereas among people who had not been given grants in the last 5 years who received scores higher than 2.0, only 5 percent received current grants.

This is an empirical illustration of the effect of accumulative advantage. Those who have succeeded in the past have a better chance of succeeding currently, independent of the measure of role performance, that is, the mean ratings of the reviewers. This is a conservative test of the influence of the accumulative advantage factor because the indicator we are using as a measure of role performance, mean rating, itself may have been influenced by the past track records of the scientists.[9]

The second part of Table 39 shows the same relationship in geophysics. Among applicants who received mean ratings of 2.0 or lower, 100 percent of former grant recipients received current grants, and 79 percent of applicants who were not former grant recipients received current grants. Among those who received mean scores above 2.0, 57 percent of former grant recipients and 28 percent of nonrecipients received grants. We have found effects of accumulative advantage from granting history in solid-state physics and, to less extent, in geophysics. It is noteworthy that there was no evidence of accumulative advantage in 7 of the 10 programs we studied.

[9]It should also be pointed out, however, that there may be significant differences in the mean ratings within each of the two categories of this variable. These differences may account for some of the observed effect of granting history.

RANK OF CURRENT DEPARTMENT

A preferred position in the social structure of science is a reward for past achievements and a resource with which to do better research. Many of the advantages of place are self-evident: to be located at a superior university provides opportunities to use superior local equipment and facilities. Facilities needed for some kinds of research are often lacking at less prestigious institutions. Thus a scientist's current location has a probable influence on his ability to obtain additional resources. Further, location in a superior research setting allows for substantial useful interaction with other scientists of quality. How much does rank of current department influence decisions at the National Science Foundation?

We asked program directors whether scientists at the top universities had an edge in the decision-making process. Critics of peer review, including some prior program directors, have claimed that some social characteristics of scientists, particularly their university affiliations, influence decisions. One former program director whom we interviewed commented on this issue:

We really felt pressure from the major institutions to fund all their people. There are schools that for 3 years we never turned down a single individual. Someone turns in a weak proposal from one of these places and gets funded and someone from [low prestige institutions] sends in a strong one and doesn't get funded. We come up against very strong pressure. . . . They expect to be funded and they let you know about it in no uncertain terms. And we're at their mercy. We've used them. They're our top reviewers and frequently they're our top ———————.

However, when another person from the same research area was asked about the preceding statement on the influence of institutional location, he said the following:

I don't have the sense that there is that pressure. Bring ——————— in and ask him if he feels that there's pressure on him when he wants to decline someone from MIT or Berkeley or a place like that. I think he'll say, "Ugh!" I don't say we wouldn't get calls, but we don't mind declining people from those schools. The fact of the matter is that we don't very often because they are high-quality schools and their people are generally very good. There are cases where we do decline people in those institutions.

We interviewed two other program directors from this section. They reported that they too had frequent contact with scientists in prestigious departments. In fact, they said that they tend to rely heavily on those scientists for advice and reviewing. Essentially, all these program directors were reporting the same matter—having contact with prestigious scientists. Where they differed, though, was in their assessment of the nature of the contact. One program director experienced it as pressure, while others viewed it as a source of useful counsel.

Data showing the influence of rank of current department on granting decisions are presented in Table 40. Column 1 shows that in 8 of the 10 programs, rank of academic department is correlated in some degree with whether or not a scientist received a grant. The two programs in which it shows no meaningful correlation are anthropology and geophysics. We conclude that in most programs, scientists currently employed at prestigious institutions do have a somewhat better chance of receiving grants (although it may not be because of their institutions) than do scientists in less prestigious departments.

Once again, an important analytic question is whether scientists located in prestigious departments have a better chance of receiving grants than do their colleagues in less prestigious departments *independently of the ratings given their proposals.*

The proportion of variance explained by the ratings of reviewers and panels, plus the rankings of scientists' current departments, is presented in column 3. For example, in algebra, the mean ratings of the reviewers explained 76 percent of the variance. When we add the rank

TABLE 40 Influence of Rank of Current Department on Decision (Probit Estimated R^2)

Program	Rank of Current Department	Mean Ratings Plus Panel Ratings	Reviewer Ratings Plus Rank of Current Department	Difference
Algebra	0.20	0.76	0.78	0.02
Anthropology	0.00	0.83	0.84	0.01
Biochemistry	0.19	0.86	0.86	0.00
Chemical Dynamics	0.12	0.91	0.93	0.02
Ecology	0.10	0.77	0.79	0.02
Economics	0.17	0.78	0.78	0.00
Fluid Mechanics	0.08	0.57	0.58	0.01
Geophysics[a]	0.05	0.49	0.49	0.00
Meteorology[a]	0.07	0.92	0.92	0.00
Solid-State Physics	0.28	0.71	0.74	0.03

[a]Rank of department scores based upon survey of NAS members (see Appendix B).

of the mathematician's department to the probit regression equation, we increase the proportion of variance explained by only 2 percent. In short, rank of department has no meaningful effect above and beyond that of reviewer ratings. If rank of department has any effect at all on funding, it works through its influence on reviewers rather than through the NSF program director and his superiors. We have already demonstrated that institutional location of applicants has only a minor influence on reviewer ratings.

PROFESSIONAL AGE

Most program directors claim that young applicants who have not had the opportunity to build track records are given special consideration. One program director specifically noted attempts to aid young scientists:

Because we try to encourage younger men in the field to get going, to get independent of their Ph.D. advisors, we do add on a few "brownie points" for being a young, new scientist.

Another program director spoke of the advantage that younger people have in the competition for funds. He said:

With young principal investigators we tend to be somewhat gentle—that given the guy has made a conscientious effort and has written quite a nice proposal, we would recommend something at a slightly lower level [mean rating] than I would a senior investigator.

This last point is important. Since the young investigator has a limited track record, if any, there is greater reliance on the content and quality of the proposal. As one program director stated:

Where the name of the young man is not going to mean much to the reviewer, there is not much that he can do about that. So how he writes his proposal has to be the main criterion.

Program directors frequently use additional information to establish or to fortify their own judgments of young people. In one program the known teachers of the young scientist, as well as his departmental affiliation, were used in reaching decisions:

You see what they published, if anything at all, you find out what their thesis advisor says about them, you try to find someone who wasn't as intimate with them as their thesis advisor, and you try to support what you consider the best of the lot.

It has also been noted that decisions made about young people are risky. One program director said:

I feel that it takes a minimum of 13 gambles to get a good payoff. You have to fund 13 people whom it's yes-no business to get one really good person, who 3 or 4 years later you can say, "I gave him his first break."

Others talked of getting "flack" for giving funds to unproven investigators, but in most cases they claimed that these gambles paid off.

Program directors frequently said that if the proposal ratings of younger and older scientists were roughly equal, they would give the edge to the younger scientists, because the older ones should have been able to construct better proposals and because the NSF had an obligation to help young scientists get started. One program director said:

Given two proposals where technically the merit would be equivalent, the bias would go to the young investigator.

In some scientific fields (according to the program director in charge) young people have almost no chance of funding. In physics, for example, many specialties are organized into large research teams, and younger scientists have little chance for independent funding:

The younger people in particle physics don't get a grant. There is no way you could set up your own group as a going enterprise and try to do experiments in particle physics. You need too much equipment, too much money, too much organization, and too much collaboration. The way young people get into it and eventually become independent is by joining existing groups.

Although most program directors suggested that youngsters actually had some advantage, some told us that the social structure of the scientific discipline precluded the funding of younger experimentalists.

To what extent do the data support the contention of many program directors that young people are given special consideration in the decision-making process? In order to analyze the influence of professional age, we divided the sample into two groups: those who received their Ph.D. degrees in 1970 or after (younger scientists) and those who received them before 1970 (older scientists). We did this because most scientists have established some track record by the time they have been out of graduate school for 5 years, and we were not interested here in the influence of variation in professional age among scientists who have already had the opportunity to establish track records. Twenty-nine percent of the applicants were classified as "young" scientists. Forty-six percent of young applicants and 54 percent of

TABLE 41   Influence of Professional Age on Decision (Probit Estimated R^2)

Program	Professional Age	Mean Rating Plus Panel Rating	Reviewer Rating Plus Age	Difference
Algebra	0.02 (−)[a]	0.76	0.80	0.04
Anthropology	0.03	0.83	0.83	0.00
Biochemistry	0.00	0.86	0.86	0.00
Chemical Dynamics	0.05	0.91	0.92	0.01
Ecology	0.02 (−)[a]	0.77	0.78	0.01
Economics	0.00	0.78	0.78	0.00
Fluid Mechanics	0.06	0.57	0.60	0.03
Geophysics	0.00	0.49	0.49	0.00
Meteorology	0.00	0.92	0.92	0.00
Solid-State Physics	0.14	0.70	0.76	0.06

[a]In these fields, young scientists had a slightly better chance of receiving grants than their older colleagues.

older applicants received grants.[10] Thus, young applicants have almost as good a chance of receiving NSF grants as do more established applicants.

Column 1 of Table 41 shows probit estimates for professional age in each of the 10 fields. A negative sign next to the estimate indicates that young people are more likely to receive grants. The only field in which young people are significantly less likely to get grants is solid-state physics. But, as the last column of Table 41 indicates, in none of the fields does age explain much additional variance after reviewer ratings are entered into the probit regression equation.

OTHER CHARACTERISTICS OF APPLICANTS

We have data for three other characteristics of principal investigators: whether they are employed at Ph.D.-granting institutions, the rankings of the departments at which they earned their doctorates, and, for

[10]Some of the younger scientists may have been coprincipal investigators with older scientists. To see whether this had any effect on the findings, we took all grants that had more than one principal investigator and, using citations to recent work as a measure of eminence, excluded all but the most eminent investigator from the analysis. We found the correlations between professional age and decision to be virtually identical to the correlations obtained when the coprincipals were included. Thus the results about age have not been significantly influenced by the inclusion of coprincipal investigators.

academic scientists, their academic ranks (full professor, associate professor, or assistant professor). In general, none of these variables had a strong influence on granting decisions. Exceptions are the influence of academic rank and the rank of the department in which the scientist earned his Ph.D. in the solid-state physics program and the influence of rank of doctoral department in the anthropology program. For descriptive purposes, we report the probit R^2 estimates for influence of these variables on decisions in Table 42.

COMBINED EFFECTS OF THE NINE CHARACTERISTICS

We have been examining the extent to which some characteristics of applicants for NSF funds influence the decisions made by program directors. In particular, we have focused on the extent to which eminent, well-established investigators located at prestigious universities have a better chance of getting grants independent of the ratings given their proposals. We shall now discuss the combined effects of the characteristics we have been studying on decision. The data are presented in Table 43.

The first column of Table 43 shows the total proportion of variance

TABLE 42   Influence of Professional Rank, Rank of Ph.D. Department, and Type of Current Institution on Decision (Probit Estimated R^2)

Program	Academic Rank	Rank of Ph.D. Department	Type of Current Institution (Ph.D.- Granting or Other)
Algebra	0.02	0.10	0.01
Anthropology	0.01	0.13	0.02
Biochemistry	0.02	0.02	0.04
Chemical Dynamics	0.06	0.08	0.07
Ecology	0.00	0.00	0.04
Economics	0.01	0.02	0.01
Fluid Mechanics	0.01	0.00	0.00
Geophysics	0.00	0.00	0.05
Meteorology	0.00	0.04[a]	0.06
Solid-State Physics	0.20	0.12	0.02

[a]The sign on this relationship is negative.

TABLE 43   Estimated Variance on Funding Decisions Explained by Characteristics of Principal Investigators and Ratings of Reviewers (Probit Estimated R^2)

Program	Nine Individual Variables[a]	Mean Rating of Reviewers (and Panels Where They Exist)	Nine Individual Variables Plus Mean Rating of Reviewers and Panels	Increase in Variance Due to Nine Individual Variables
Algebra	0.34	0.76	0.84	0.08
Anthropology	0.17	0.83	0.86	0.03
Biochemistry	0.51	0.86	0.86	0.00
Chemical Dynamics	0.39	0.92	0.96	0.04
Ecology	0.40	0.77	0.86	0.09
Economics	0.39	0.78	0.83	0.05
Fluid Mechanics	0.37	0.58	0.71	0.13
Geophysics	0.34	0.49	0.65	0.16
Meteorology	0.24	0.92	0.94	0.02
Solid-State Physics	0.70	0.70	0.91	0.21

[a]The variables include rank of Ph.D. department, professional age, rank of current department, academic rank, log of citations to work published in last 10 years, log of citations to work published more than 10 years ago, log of papers published in last 10 years, whether or not employed in a Ph.D.-granting institution, number of years funded between 1970 and 1974. We excluded in each field those variables that had negative correlation with decision. These were professional age in algebra, ecology, and meteorology; productivity in economics; and rank of doctoral department of meteorology.

explained by the nine characteristics for which we have data.[11] Essentially these characteristics describe the statuses of applicants in the stratification system of science as measured by their past productivity and the current rankings of their departments. They also include their granting histories with the NSF, the rankings of their doctoral departments, professional ages, and academic ranks.

The nine characteristics explain different amounts of variance in grant decisions in the different programs, from a low of 17 percent in anthropology to a high of 70 percent in solid-state physics (column 1 of Table 43). The significant finding, however, is not how much total variance is explained by these variables but how much additional variance above that explained by peer review ratings alone is explained by these variables. That is, when we add the nine variables to a probit

[11]For a comparison of these results with those obtained from ordinary least squares analysis, see Appendix B.

regression equation in which we have already entered the ratings of peer reviewers, how much does the estimated R^2 increase?

Column 3 of Table 43 shows the total proportions of variance explained by a combination of all the variables, the ratings of the peer reviewers, and the nine characteristics. In column 4, we have subtracted the number in column 2 from the number in column 3, that is, the proportion explained by peer review ratings alone from the proportion explained by the combination of peer review ratings and principal investigator characteristics.

Clearly, in most of the programs we have studied, the characteristics of principal investigators add relatively little to the proportion of explained variance in decisions with three exceptions. The first is geophysics. We have already explained why geophysics is difficult to deal with. Because we do not have data on the panel ratings, it is very difficult to determine the extent to which the individual characteristics of geophysicist applicants influence the program director's decision. However, following the same logic used above, it appears to us that if we did have data on the panel ratings, the total proportion of variance explained by the individual characteristics of the principal investigators would not add much to the proportion explained by the ratings of mail reviewers and panel reviewers. This, however, must remain speculative. The two programs that show the most influence of the characteristics of principal investigators are fluid mechanics and solid-state physics. The nine individual characteristics explained an additional 13 percent of the variance in fluid mechanics and an additional 21 percent of the variance in solid-state physics.

In general, program directors' funding decisions are not heavily influenced by the characteristics of applicants beyond the effects of those characteristics on ratings.

INFLUENCE OF GEOGRAPHIC LOCATION ON DECISIONS

The congressional act regulating the NSF states that the organization should "avoid undue concentration" of research funds. As noted in the introduction to this report, the NSF states that when the assessed quality of applications is roughly equal, geographic location is considered in making decisions. The NSF policy on geographic location is stated in the staff study entitled "Peer Review and Proposal Evaluation" (June 1975, Appendix I, pp. 7-8).

In the general competition for basic research grants, our policy has always been that, where a selection must be made from a group of projects of substantially equal merit, we will select those which contribute to the avoidance of undue concentration. This policy we attempt to apply uniformly in all programs. It should not be interpreted as meaning that projects must be strictly matched on an "all-other-things-being-equal" basis. Rather, we should think in terms of a quality band or cut-off zone within which a considerable number of projects may be considered as having substantially equal merit. Within that cut-off zone selections should look both to geographical distribution and to distribution by type of academic institution.

The NSF presented a document to the House subcommittee investigating peer review in which they showed that with the exception of a few states (Massachusetts, New York, the District of Columbia, and California), the distribution of awards to the states matched closely the distribution of population, scientists, and eminent scientists.[12]

We have divided the 1,200 applicants we studied into East, South, Midwest, and West.[13] We found that the proposals of 55 percent of eastern applicants, 35 percent of southern applicants, 51 percent of midwestern applicants, and 60 percent of western applicants were approved. The fact that the percentage of approvals of southern applicants was smaller than the others does not mean that they were discriminated against. The lower ratings could result from either the lower perceived quality of their proposals or the difference between track records and other characteristics of southern applicants and those of applicants from other areas of the country. In fact, as the data in Table 13 suggest, in 7 of the 10 programs, applicants from the South received poorer mean ratings than applicants from the other sections.

The more relevant question is how applicants from the different sections have fared when their proposals received roughly equal peer review ratings. Since we had too few cases in each program to analyze the effect of region for each program, we have combined the data from

[12]This appears in National Science Foundation, *An Analysis of the Geographical Distribution of NSF Awards as Compared with Other Selected Indicators*, 1975c. The figures in this report are based upon the distribution of NSF funds in all divisions.
[13]The groupings are: East—Maine, New Hampshire, Vermont, Massachusetts, Rhode Island, Connecticut, New York, New Jersey, Pennsylvania, Delaware, Maryland, and District of Columbia. South—Virginia, West Virginia, North Carolina, South Carolina, Georgia, Florida, Alabama, Tennessee, Kentucky, Arkansas, Mississippi, Louisiana, and Texas. Midwest—Ohio, Michigan, Indiana, Illinois, Wisconsin, Minnesota, Iowa, Missouri, Oklahoma, Kansas, Nebraska, South Dakota, and North Dakota. West—Montana, Wyoming, Colorado, Idaho, Utah, New Mexico, Arizona, Nevada, California, Oregon, Washington, Alaska, and Hawaii.

TABLE 44 Influence of Region on Funding Decision: All Fields Combined (Standardized Data)^a

Mean Peer Review Ratings, % Receiving Grants

Region	High		Borderline		Low	
East	95	(139)	52	(125)	10	(117)
South	92	(36)	43	(51)	1	(73)
Midwest	86	(93)	52	(121)	11	(90)
West	94	(116)	61	(94)	15	(87)

Mean Peer Review Ratings Averaged Over Group

| Region | High | | Borderline | | Low | |
	Accepted	Declinations	Accepted	Declinations	Accepted	Declinations
East	-1.06 (132)	-0.93 (7)	-0.14 (65)	-0.03 (60)	0.70 (12)	1.22 (105)
South	-1.07 (33)	-0.80 (3)	-0.14 (22)	-0.03 (29)	0.72 (1)	1.23 (72)
Midwest	-1.02 (80)	-0.87 (13)	-0.18 (63)	-0.02 (58)	0.86 (10)	1.22 (80)
West	-1.08 (109)	-0.85 (7)	-0.13 (57)	-0.09 (37)	0.80 (13)	1.15 (74)

Numbers of applicants are in parentheses.

^{a}The Z-score transformations used to standardize the data produced a distribution of ratings within each program with a mean of 0 and a standard deviation of 1. The standardized scores were then combined for all 10 NSF programs studied. The cell entries in the lower table are standardized rating. Here the "lower" the number, the "higher" the rating.

all 10 programs and based the analysis upon the standardized data. We have divided the transformed scores for the mean peer review ratings into three groups: those receiving relatively high ratings, those receiving relatively low ratings, and those receiving ratings in the middle of the distribution, or borderline cases. In Table 44 we show the proportion of applicants from each region who received grants in each of the three mean rating categories. For example, among applicants who received relatively high peer review ratings on their proposals, 95 percent from the East, 92 percent from the South, 86 percent from the Midwest, and 94 percent from the West received grants. Among those whose proposals fell into the borderline area, 52 percent from the East, 43 percent from the South, 52 percent from the Midwest, and 61 percent from the West received grants. Among applicants whose proposals received relatively low peer review ratings, 10 percent from the East, 1 percent from the South, 11 percent from the Midwest, and 15 percent from the West received grants. These data indicate that applicants from the South are slightly less likely to receive NSF grants even when their ratings are similar to those of applicants from other sections of the country.

It is still possible that there could be significant differences within each of the three rating categories in Table 44 for applicants coming from the different sections, that is, it is possible that southern applicants in the borderline area may have received slightly less favorable peer review ratings than eastern applicants in the borderline cases. To check this possibility, we present the data in the bottom of Table 44. In this part of the table we have once again divided the applicants by region and by the three groups of mean peer review ratings. However, in the cells of the table we show the average rating received by applicants whose proposals were approved and those whose proposals were declined. We are particularly interested in comparing southern applicants in the borderline and low categories with applicants in these categories from other sections of the country.

Let us begin with applicants in the borderline category. The statistics on declination in the borderline category show that, on the average, proposals of southern applicants that were declined received just about the same mean ratings as did those of applicants in the other three sections that were declined. The data on those who received relatively low peer review ratings show the same thing, that is, that southern applicants who are declined receive just about the same ratings on their proposals as the applicants from the other sections who are declined. The effect observed in the borderline and low categories is not very large. These data lead to the tentative conclusion that geographic location of applicants has very little, if any, effect on decisions.

Several cautions must be exercised in interpreting these data. First, we have combined the data from all 10 programs into 1 sample. It is possible that in some programs, geographic region is given more consideration than in others. It is also possible that the slight differences we have observed are a result of variables not measured in this study.

AMOUNT OF MONEY APPLIED FOR AND FUNDING DECISIONS

Many observers of the peer review system believe that the size of a project's budget influences its chances for funding. Principal investigators may try to shape their budgets with this belief in mind. Tailoring the budget size to the overall budget of an NSF program is surely required. Information about "ball park" budget figures is often obtained through informal communication between scientists and program officers. Data from the qualitative interviews attest to this fact. These contacts produce some restrictions on the range in budgets submitted to the Foundation. But how much does variation in budget size among submitted proposals affect final decisions? For the more than 1,000 proposals we have studied, we have data on the total amount of money requested.

Using the decision as the dependent variable, we computed probit estimates of the influence of amount of money applied for. Table 45 shows that in no field does the amount of requested funds noticeably

TABLE 45 Influence of Amount of Money Requested on Decision (Probit Estimated R^2): 10 Programs

Program	Estimated R^2
Algebra	0.12
Anthropology	0.01[a]
Biochemistry	0.04
Chemical Dynamics	0.01[a]
Ecology	0.00
Economics	0.00
Fluid Mechanics	0.00
Geophysics	0.04
Meteorology	0.10
Solid-State Physics	0.10

[a]Sign on relationship is negative.

hurt the chances of obtaining an NSF award. In only 2 of the 10 fields, anthropology and chemical dynamics, is there a negative correlation between the amount requested and the decision, and in these fields the associations are so weak that the estimated variance explained thereby is not significantly more than zero. The only estimates worth noting—those in algebra, meteorology, and solid-state physics—indicate that larger projects are more apt than smaller ones to be given awards.

We thought that, although the amount of money applied for had no negative influence on decisions among all the applicants to a program, it might have an influence on decisions for those who had not applied for NSF funds in the last 5 years. We therefore conducted the analysis separately for this group. The analysis showed that even among the applicants in this group, practically all of them new NSF applicants, those who applied for relatively large amounts of money had just as good chances of getting grants as those who applied for relatively little money.[14]

TABULAR ANALYSIS OF DATA ON DECISION

As we pointed out in section 3, regression analysis tells us the extent to which particular characteristics of the applicant enable us to predict ratings received from peer reviewers. Earlier in this section, we used probit analysis when decision was the dependent variable. This technique, however, does not allow us to make direct comparisons among people with distinctly different characteristics. In order to do this, we have used tabular analysis. The problem in using tabular analysis for decision is, as was pointed out above, that in most programs we have approximately 120 cases. This is too small a sample size to permit an accurate evaluation of the characteristics affecting decision. Therefore we treated applicants in all 10 programs in a combined sample. We standardized the data separately within each program and then analyzed the data using standardized scores instead of the absolute scores.[15]

In assessing the results to be presented below the reader must remember that we have combined the data from all 10 programs. As we have already pointed out, all programs do not operate in the same way. For example, in some programs younger investigators have an advan-

---

[14]Because of small numbers of cases in each program, this analysis treated the entire sample as a unit after standardizing amounts applied for separately for each program. The probit equation was then computed using the standard scores.

[15]For a description of the standardization procedure employed, see section 3, pages 53-54.

TABLE 46   Influence of Mail Ratings on Decision

	Percent Receiving Grants			
Mean Rating of			Panel Programs	
Mail Reviewers	All Programs		Excluded	
High	92	(382)	95	(239)
Medium	52	(384)	52	(259)
Low	10	(390)	9	(221)

Numbers of applicants are in parentheses.

tage while in other programs they are at some disadvantage. Likewise, in some programs the number of citations is fairly strongly associated with the granting decision, while in other programs there is little or no association between the two. These differences are blurred when we combine the data from all 10 programs into 1 sample. Nonetheless, the tabular analysis presented below does allow us to compare scientists with different characteristics.

Table 46 shows the relationship between the mean rating given a proposal by mail reviewers and the decision. Since the mean ratings were standardized separately within each field, we have roughly divided them into high, medium, and low groups. The first column of Table 46 shows that 92 percent of those proposals given high mean ratings by mail reviewers were funded. Among those given low mean ratings by mail reviewers only 10 percent were funded. Approximately half of the proposals given medium mean ratings were funded. The second column of Table 46 shows the same relationship; however, this time, data from the fields employing panels were excluded.[16] In those fields the opinions of mail reviewers and panels may differ and program directors may be influenced by the panels. When we excluded panel fields, we found an even stronger relationship between the ratings of mail reviewers and decisions. Now 95 percent of proposals receiving high ratings are funded, and only 9 percent of those receiving low ratings are funded.

Among the fields not using panels, 53 percent of the proposals were funded. Therefore, if without any information we had to guess whether or not a proposal was funded or not funded, we would be correct in 53

[16]In this section of the analysis we have treated geophysics as a nonpanel field, since we do not have any data on the panel ratings. When geophysicists were excluded from the data presented in column 2 of Table 46, we found that, among applicants receiving high mean ratings, 95 percent were awarded grants; among those receiving median mean ratings, 49 percent; and among those receiving low mean ratings, 5 percent.

TABLE 47   Influence of Panel Ratings on Decision (Only Fields with Panels)

Mean Rating of Panel Members	Percent Receiving Grants	
High	84	(99)
Medium	52	(163)
Low	12	(144)

Numbers of applicants are in parentheses.

percent of the cases. Using knowledge of the trichotomized mean rating score we can guess correctly in 78 percent of the cases, an increase of 25 percentage points.[17]

Despite the fact that mean ratings by mail reviewers are so highly associated with decisions, we were still interested in those few deviant cases in which decisions did not correspond with the mean ratings. We listed all proposals in each field according to the mean ratings they received, with the "best" proposals at the top and the "worst" proposals at the bottom. We then looked at which were funded and which not funded. We were then able to identify cases in which decisions did not closely correspond to the mean ratings by mail reviewers. In half of these cases it turned out that there was a difference of opinion between the panel and the mail reviewers and the program director went along with the panel. We are still analyzing the other half to see if we can detect any systematic pattern among these cases in which the reviews did not determine the decision. Thus far, our analysis suggests that those who benefit from such discretionary decisions are slightly more apt to be eminent scientists, but once again the effect is small.

Table 47 presents the relationship between mean rating given a proposal by panel members (for those fields employing panels) and the decision. The association is strong, and the cases in which panel ratings are not in agreement with the decision could easily be cases in which

[17]This "modal" guessing maximizes the number of correct guesses both for prediction from the marginals and for prediction within the categories of the independent variable. "Proportional prediction" that would have reproduced the marginal totals on the dependent variable (Leo Goodman and William Krusal, "Measures of Association in Cross-Classification II," *Journal of the American Statistical Association*, vol. 54, 1959, pp. 123-163) could also have been used. This would have lowered the proportion of correct guesses in both conditions, but their relative magnitudes (in this case 0.502 and 0.71) would have remained approximately the same. This more complex procedure would have been necessary had the mode of the dependent variable been in the same category for each category of the independent variable. Since this was not the case, we chose to use the simpler procedure.

mail reviewers and panel members disagreed and the program director went along with the mail reviewers.

In Table 48 we have divided the 1,200 applicants in the 10 different programs according to the standardized score on the number of citations to recent work. We divided them roughly into quintiles and then examined the proportion in each quintile that received grants. In the highest quintile, 78 percent received grants, and in the lowest quintile, 30 percent received grants. Since a total of 51 percent of the 1,200 proposals were funded, without any additional information we could guess the outcome correctly in 51 percent of the cases. With the citation information presented in Table 48 we could guess whether a project was funded or declined in 63 percent of the cases, or an increase of 12 percentage points.

As one would expect, investigators who have been successful in the past, as indicated by citations to their work, have a better chance of receiving an NSF grant than do those who have not been successful in the past. The effect is considerably larger at the extremes than it is in the middle of the distribution. But even at the extremes the number of citations to one's past work does not completely determine whether or not one receives a grant. Twenty-two percent of those whose work was most cited did not receive grants, and 30 percent of those whose work was least cited did receive grants. Thus, these data lead us to conclude that citations to one's work are moderately correlated with success in getting an NSF grant. We know that citations have some influence on ratings of proposals and that the ratings have a major influence on the decisions of program directors. Perhaps the most significant question is: To what extent are program directors influenced in their decision making by the characteristics of the applicants conditional on fixed values of the scores they receive from peer reviewers. In order to answer this question we must examine a three-variable table in which we look at the proportion receiving grants in different citation

TABLE 48   Influence of Citations in 1974 to Work Published between 1965-1974 on Decision (All Fields Combined)

Number of Citations Received	Percent Receiving Grants	
High	78	(239)
	58	(239)
Medium	50	(238)
	41	(240)
Low	30	(244)

Numbers of applicants are in parentheses.

TABLE 49   Influence of Reviewers by Citations in 1974 to Work Published between 1965 and 1974 on Decision, Controlling for Mean Rating (All Fields Combined)

Citations to Work Published in 1965-1974	Percent Receiving Grants					
	High Mean Rating of Reviewers		Medium Mean Rating of Reviewers		Low Mean Rating of Reviewers	
High	99	(136)	60	(54)	32	(41)
	92	(91)	58	(77)	9	(69)
Medium	90	(61)	55	(92)	10	(78)
	86	(50)	49	(85)	11	(97)
Low	78	(44)	41	(76)	2	(110)

Numbers of applicants are in parentheses.

categories while controlling for peer review ratings. (See Table 49.) Table 49 shows that peer review ratings are far more important than citations in determining whether or not a proposal will be funded.

For example, the data on applicants in the highest quintile of citations show that the mean ratings they received on their proposals had a very strong effect on success in getting grants; with 99 percent of those receiving the highest ratings and 32 percent of those receiving the lowest ratings (a 67-point percentage difference) receiving grants. On the other hand, for applicants who received high ratings on their proposals, citations had a relatively slight influence on success in getting grants, with 99 percent of people in the highest citation category and 78 percent of people in the lowest citation category (a 21-point percentage difference) receiving grants. Further, scientists with the highest numbers of citations who receive medium ratings on their proposals are less likely to receive grants than are those with the lowest numbers of citations who receive high ratings.

The data in Table 49 are somewhat misleading, since they include data from fields employing panels. Panel judgments sometimes differ from those of mail reviewers and thus create the impression that the peer reviews were not the determining influence on decisions. Table 50 is identical to Table 49, except that it includes only those fields not employing panels. This table demonstrates even more clearly that, when ratings of proposals are controlled, citations have very little if any meaningful effect on the likelihood of receiving a grant. The only exception is in the lowest citation category for people whose proposals were highly rated. People in the very lowest citation quintile are somewhat less likely than people in the higher quintiles to receive grants even if they received high ratings. For people receiving medium

TABLE 50 Influence of Reviewers by Citations in 1974 to Work Published between 1965 and 1974 on Decision Controlling for Mean Rating (Excluding Panel Fields; All Fields Combined)

Citations to Work Published in 1965-1974	Percent Receiving Grants					
	High Mean Rating of Reviewers		Medium Mean Rating of Reviewers		Low Mean Rating of Reviewers	
High	100	(90)	53	(34)	16	(19)
	93	(59)	57	(56)	10	(40)
Medium	95	(40)	57	(62)	8	(48)
	96	(24)	49	(51)	14	(50)
Low	77	(26)	43	(56)	3	(64)

Numbers of applicants are in parentheses.

or low ratings on their proposals, citations make virtually no difference in the probability of success. The data presented in this table show that citations to the work of applicants, here being used as an indicator of the extent to which their past scientific work has been highly evaluated by the scientific community, have very little if any independent effect on decisions of program directors beyond the effect, already taken into account, of reviewer ratings.

The data from the tabular analysis show that applicants whose proposals receive high ratings almost invariably receive grants and that applicants whose proposals receive low ratings almost invariably do not receive grants, regardless of other applicant characteristics we have studied. The data also indicate that applicants whose proposals receive ratings in the middle have about a 50 percent chance of receiving grants. We have been interested to know what determines grant decisions when the peer review ratings fall into this middle category. At first we thought that when peer review ratings did not provide a sufficient basis for discriminating among proposals, program directors might rely upon the characteristics of applicants and their institutions in making decisions. However, as the data in Table 50 suggest, the characteristics of the applicants, in this case citations, have no greater effect in the middle category of ratings than they do in the two extreme categories. Thus far we have not been able to find any systematic determinant of decision when the peer review scores fall into the borderline area. Apparently, these decisions depended more heavily on the judgment of the program director. Further research is necessary on how decisions are made when the peer review ratings fall into the borderline area.

TABLE 51 Influence of Citations Made in 1974 to Work Published Prior to 1965 on Decision (All Fields Combined)

Citations to Work Published Prior to 1965[a]	Percent Receiving Grants	
High	77	(86)
	69	(86)
Medium	64	(86)
Low	49	(86)
None	46	(856)

Numbers of applicants are in parentheses.
[a]For this table all applicants who had zero citations in 1974 to work published prior to 1965 were placed in the bottom category, and the remaining cases were divided into quartiles using the Z scores.

Tables 51 and 52 show the influence of citations to older work and of numbers of papers published in the last 10 years on the probability of receiving grants. Both these variables have a relatively minor effect on this probability beyond that of ratings by reviewers.

Table 53 shows the influence of rank of an applicant's current department or institution on the probability of receiving an award. Applicants from highly ranked departments are more likely to receive NSF grants than those from lowly ranked departments or from unranked or nonacademic institutions. Without any information we are able to predict 51 percent of the cases correctly. With information on rank of the applicant's current department we can predict 64 percent of the cases correctly, an increase of 13 percentage points in predictability. Here too, however, we are primarily interested in the independent influence of rank of department on decision after we have controlled for mean reviewer ratings of proposals. These data are presented in Table 54. In this table we have excluded data in fields employing

TABLE 52 Influence of Number of Papers Published between 1965 and 1974 on Decision (All Fields Combined)

Number of Papers Published between 1965 and 1974	Percent Receiving Grants	
High	62	(238)
	59	(242)
Medium	53	(240)
	44	(239)
Low	41	(241)

Numbers of applicants are in parentheses.

TABLE 53   Influence of Rank of Current Department on Decision (All Fields Combined)

Rank of Current Department[a]	Percent Receiving Grants	
High	74	(242)
Medium	56	(150)
	61	(175)
Low	43	(171)
Unranked and nonacademic	38	(462)
Gamma = 0.39		

Numbers of applicants are in parentheses.
[a]We have used nonstandardized rank of department scores.

TABLE 54   Influence of Rank of Present Department on Decision Controlling for Mean Rating of Reviewers (Excluding Panel Fields; All Fields Combined)

Rank of Present Department[a]	Percent Receiving Grants					
	High Mean Rating of Mail Reviewers		Medium Mean Rating of Mail Reviewers		Low Mean Rating of Mail Reviewers	
High	94	(86)	58	(38)	6	(18)
	100	(32)	62	(34)	4	(25)
Medium	96	(49)	58	(60)	29	(38)
Low	94	(31)	53	(49)	7	(44)
Unranked and nonacademic	90	(41)	38	(78)	4	(96)

Numbers of applicants are in parentheses.
[a]We have used nonstandardized rank of department scores.

panels. The data in Table 54 indicate that, when we control for the mean rating of mail reviewers, rank of an applicant's department has virtually no influence on success in getting grants beyond that of reviewer ratings.[18]

The only exception to this is among applicants whose proposals receive medium ratings and who are located at unranked or nonacademic institutions. These applicants are somewhat less likely to receive grants than those receiving similar ratings on their proposals

[18]Note the 29 percent figure for middle department ranking in the last column, which is very much greater than the percentages for both highest and lowest departments. This shows that the assumption of linearity in regression and probit analysis probably does not hold here. However, to substantiate this, it would be necessary to have several different samples showing the same results, because these percentages are based on a small number of cases.

TABLE 55   Influence of Type of Institution on Decision
(All Fields Combined)

Type of Current Institution	Percent Receiving Grants	
Ph.D.-granting	55	(922)
Other	40	(278)

Numbers of applicants are in parentheses.

who are located in ranked graduate departments. However, among applicants who get either high ratings or low ratings, rank of department has no independent influence on the decisions of program directors.

Table 55 shows the influence on decisions of the institution at which an applicant is located. Scientists at Ph.D.-granting institutions are slightly more likely than those at non-Ph.D.-granting institutions to receive NSF grants.

Tables 56, 57, and 58 present the effects of rank of Ph.D. department, academic rank, and professional age on decision. Each of these variables has relatively little effect on the probability of receiving a grant.

Table 59 shows the influence of NSF funding history on decision. We have divided the applicants into those who have received NSF funds in the previous 5-year period and those who have not. Among those who have been funded by the NSF in the past 5 years, 65 percent were awarded grants on their current applications, whereas among those who had not received any NSF support in the previous 5 years, 40 percent were awarded NSF grants on their current applications. Again, a question of primary significance is the extent to which NSF granting history has an effect on the decision beyond that of the mean

TABLE 56   Influence of Rank of Ph.D. Department on Decision
(All Fields Combined)[a]

Rank of Ph.D. Department	Percent Receiving Grants	
High	62	(374)
	54	(279)
Medium	49	(138)
Low	38	(93)
Unranked and no information	42	(316)

Numbers of applicants are in parentheses.
[a]We have used nonstandardized rank of department scores.

TABLE 57 Influence of Academic Rank on Decision (All Fields Combined)

Academic Rank	Percent Receiving Grants	
Assistant professor	45	(281)
Associate professor	49	(303)
Full professor	58	(488)

Numbers of applicants are in parentheses.

TABLE 58 Influence of Professional Age on Decision (All Fields Combined)

Professional Age	Percent Receiving Grants	
Received Ph.D. before 1970	54	(873)
Received Ph.D. after 1970	46	(285)

Numbers of applicants are in parentheses.

TABLE 59 Influence of Funding History on Decision (Excluding Panel Fields; All Fields Combined)

Funded by NSF in Last 5 Years	Percent Receiving Grants	
Yes	65	(557)
No	40	(643)

Numbers of applicants are in parentheses.

rating received by the proposal. The data are presented in Table 60, in which we have excluded data on applicants in programs employing panels. The data indicate that NSF funding history does have a slight independent effect on the decision. For example, among applicants who received high ratings on their proposals and who have been funded previously, 98 percent were funded on their current applications. This compares with 89 percent who received similarly high ratings but who had not been funded in the past 5-year period. We found similar differences among applicants whose proposals received medium ratings and low ratings. In every case, applicants who had previously been funded by NSF had a slightly greater chance of being funded on their current applications.

The tabular analysis of the aggregated data on decision leads us to conclude that the primary determinant of whether an individual receives an NSF grant is peer review ratings, from both mail reviewers

TABLE 60 Influence of Number of Years Funded by NSF in Last 5 Years on Decision, Controlling for Mean Rating of Reviewers (Excluding Panel Fields; All Fields Combined)

Funded by NSF in Last 5 Years	Percent Receiving Grants					
	High Mean Rating of Reviewers		Medium Mean Rating of Reviewers		Low Mean Rating of Reviewers	
Yes	98	(148)	61	(137)	16	(81)
No	89	(91)	41	(122)	5	(140)

Numbers of applicants are in parentheses.

and panels. Scientists who are highly ranked in the social stratification system of sciences are slightly more likely to receive NSF grants than those who are ranked lower; but most of the influence of eminence on decision is through its influence on the ratings rather than its influence on the program directors. In general, program directors are not substantially influenced by those characteristics of applicants that we have studied independently of the ratings given the proposals.

Post-Decision-Making Activities of the Program Director

HANDLING DECLINATIONS

The work of the program director is not finished when the funding decision has been made. He negotiates further with those who have been funded, and he must notify those who have been declined.

The Foundation has a standard form letter that goes out to declinees, but many program directors go beyond this. One program director described the situation in the following way:

On a declination, I feel that the principal investigators warrant an explanation. So, I have phoned every guy and warned him that the declination is coming and gave him the reasons why his proposal is going to be declined.

Program directors offer explanations for two reasons. First, the principal investigator wants to know what went wrong—what was substantively wrong with the proposal. Second, such an action signifies that the program director is sensitive to the principal investigator's disappointment in not being funded. Well-constructed peer reviews are helpful in explaining to applicants why they were not funded, and applicants can now request the verbatim comments of the peers.

As soon as we sent out the reject letters, the calls started coming in from applicants asking why they didn't get funded. The good reviewers really helped. They really provided constructive feedback to the applicants.

The feedback to applicants who have been turned down has significant implications for their future research activities. Program directors can help turned down applicants, especially those close to the cutting point, improve their chances for future awards. One said:

A couple of times, I counseled a principal investigator who was declined on how to rewrite it, to include different kinds of data, to express it in different ways. He would need to run one more experiment in this area and then resubmit it.

Further, an expression of interest by the program director can prevent applicants from believing that there is no way for them to obtain NSF grants. Program directors can in this way influence the process of self-selection into and out of the pool of applicants.

Declinations can have different implications, since some people are declined but are given explicit or implicit information that they have a good chance to be funded in the future. Others are declined and given no relevant information, and still others are declined and given information that would lead them to believe that they would have little chance of success with a resubmission.

Program directors reported varying amounts of dissatisfaction among rejected applicants. In some cases, principal investigators felt that proposals had not been properly reviewed. One case was described in the following way:

I had one bad experience with a guy who felt he had been unfairly treated. He claimed that I picked reviewers that were not familiar with his work. I asked him who he would have picked, and he named guys I had picked. He was arguing that the NSF had something against him. I worked it out with him and he eventually said that he understood the situation.

One program director talked about how a negative decision occasionally gets validated. He said:

The only thrill I've had in this job so far is when you decline a guy and he thanks you for doing it. One guy said to me, "I just want to tell you that if I had been you, I would have done exactly the same thing. I'm going back to rethink it and I appreciate the reviewers' comments."

Many program directors point out that decreases in available funds have forced them to decline proposals that would have been approved in the past. One program director said:

I wish I could write letters outlining the reasons for declination because the implication would be that every time I decline something I have a clear reason for doing it. But that's the case in a very small proportion of proposals. Most are declined because the money wouldn't go that far.

Such cases are difficult for program directors because the proposed science would probably turn out to be pretty good work. This makes it hard for the program director to explain to a rejected applicant why he has not been funded.

An additional concern of program directors is handling declinations of eminent investigators. Eminent scientists whose proposals are declined are sometimes treated differently from less prominent scientists. First, greater attention tends to be given declinations of eminent scientists. Program directors make sure that there is a superabundance of documentation because they are more concerned about the way the decision would be reviewed by superordinates in the Foundation hierarchy. Second, careful diplomacy is used in informing the individual of the declination. In short, the process of rejecting applications is apt to be more elaborate for eminent scientists than for relatively unknown ones.

Some program directors also voiced concern about turning down eminent scientists because of possible repercussions within the scientific community. Since the scientific discipline they represent is, for many program directors, at least as important a reference group as the NSF, they feel accountable not only to their superordinates within the Foundation but also to their constituencies in the science community.

Reactions of eminent scientists to declinations vary. Some take such decisions in stride and resubmit new proposals that are approved; others attempt to put pressure on the program director. One described it this way:

There are cases where a principal investigator goes to a higher up in his university and he calls my superior in the Foundation. I don't know if they are trying to imply if I don't fund them they will take it higher.

Another person talked about a conflict that he was presently involved in over this issue. He said:

I have a case where I'm having warfare with my division director over this issue. He recommended that I fund, and I didn't want to fund it. He recommended that I fund because, "He is a marvelous guy, he is a scholar, you really can't turn him down." I gave my director the reasons and it's still unresolved.

NEGOTIATING BUDGETS

The program director also has important negotiating to do with the successful grantee. This negotiation centers on the amount of money that the principal investigator will receive from the Foundation.

Applicants are required to submit budgets with their proposals specifying how they are going to use any funds they receive. After a proposal has been accepted, the program director usually confers with the principal investigator about what the "revised" budget will be. In most cases, the revised budget will be less than the original request. There are essentially two reasons for this reduction: First, because of a general decline in resources, the program director must attempt to spread available funds around. Second, the program director must consider how much "fat" there may be in a proposed budget. One program director spoke at length about what is involved in this consideration:

You look for things like the amount of foreign travel that they might ask for (you figure that's padded), secretarial assistance, administrative assistance— people that are not crucial to the experiment—(and if that's in there to a large degree, we figure that's padding), and the amount of computing time they ask for, especially if we know that there is a reasonable possibility that they can go to their dean and get free time. Ultimately, I leave it up to them. We don't tell them how to do the work, we just say, "You've asked for $60,000 and I've got $40,000—Do you feel you can rewrite the budget in a way where you can do the work within that $40,000?" By and large, they will say yes.

To put this discussion of budgetary negotiation into proper perspective, let us consider how the characteristics of investigators are related to the amount and proportion of money received. The data presented in this report suggest that the characteristics of individual scientists have little effect on the ratings of proposals and on funding decisions. Critics of the peer review system have asserted that prominent scientists in lofty positions in the social system of science are more apt than their less-distinguished colleagues to receive large grants from the Foundation. We have reported above that there is no significant relationship between the amount of money scientists apply for and funding decisions. Now we want to look only at successful applicants—those who have been funded. In each of the 10 programs, these number roughly 60.

Table 61 presents the relationship between several of the characteristics of principal investigators who received funds and the amounts of money they received.[1] Consider the general pattern of findings in the

---

[1]This analysis did not require probit estimates, since the dependent variable—amount of money received—does not have a restricted range. Therefore, we used standard Pearsonian correlation techniques. The proportion of variance explained by each variable would be the square of the correlation coefficient.

TABLE 61 Zero-Order Pearsonian Correlation Coefficients between Characteristics of Scientists on Funded NSF Research Projects and the Amount of Funds Received

Characteristics of Scientists	Program									Solid-State Physics
	Algebra	Anthropology	Biochemistry	Chemical Dynamics	Ecology	Economics	Fluid Mechanics	Geophysics	Meteorology	
Professional age	0.29	-0.28	0.12	0.14	0.28	0.25	0.24	0.11	0.06	0.12
Rank of current department	0.36	-0.24	0.24	0.25	0.33	-0.15	0.41	0.24	0.05	0.35
Citations (log of citations to work published 1965-1974)	0.23	0.26	0.51	0.23	0.08	0.14	0.15	0.07	0.24	0.33
Productivity (log of papers published 1965-1974)	0.11	0.01	0.40	0.30	0.19	0.05	0.17	-0.10	0.23	0.16
Years funded 1970-1974	0.45	-0.14	0.34	0.11	0.20	-0.05	0.31	0.01	0.25	-0.02
Mean rating	0.12	0.15	0.30	-0.03	0.00	0.11	0.08	0.24	0.32	0.35

10 programs. We begin with the professional age of principal investigators. Although the zero-order correlations differ somewhat in the several programs, the pattern suggests that senior scientists are, in fact, more apt to receive larger sums of money. Anthropology is the only program of the 10 that does not hold to this pattern.

The same pattern is found for the relationship between rank of current department and amounts received. Anthropology and economics are the only exceptions to the finding that scientists at the more prestigious universities receive more funds. In all 10 programs there is an association between the number of citations to a scientist's work and the amount of money he receives. Similarly, the level of scientific productivity, the granting history, and the mean rating of proposals are related to the amount of funds in such a way as to confirm the argument that, among scientists who are funded, those located in the upper strata of the stratification system generally receive larger grants.

To find out whether the more prominent scientists are favored in the amounts of funds they received independent of the sizes of their enterprises, we examined the proportions of funds requested that were actually received by principal investigators. If the scientists who are most prominent are also favored, we should find that they receive larger proportions of their requests. Table 62 presents the data relevant to this question. Again we present zero-order Pearsonian correlation coefficients between the same set of characteristics of the scientists and the proportions of funds requested that were received. Comparison of the associations in this table with those in Table 61 reveals a significant shift in the pattern of associations. There continues to be a small effect of the mean ratings of proposals on the proportion of funds received, but the correlations are somewhat less than we might expect. Among projects funded, some projects receiving relatively low peer review ratings ask for large sums of money and receive large proportions of the requests. Correlatively, some higher-rated proposals receive lower proportions of the requested funds than do lower-rated proposals. This raises the question of whether the amounts of requested money not given to the higher-rated projects relate to fat in the budgets, or the need to spread funds around to other, less-well-regarded projects.

In 8 of the 10 programs, young principal investigators receive a higher proportion of requested funds than do their older colleagues. In most programs, rank of current department has either a negative correlation or a very small positive correlation with proportion of funds received. Biochemistry is the only program in which highly cited principal investigators were significantly more likely to receive a high

TABLE 62 Zero-Order Pearsonian Correlation Coefficients between Characteristics of Scientists on Funded NSF Research Projects and the Proportion of Requested Budget Actually Received

Characteristics of Scientists	Program									Solid-State Physics
	Algebra	Anthropology	Biochemistry	Chemical Dynamics	Ecology	Economics	Fluid Mechanics	Geophysics	Meteorology	
Professional age	0.24	-0.17	-0.19	-0.32	-0.12	-0.28	-0.16	-0.11	-0.02	0.13
Rank of current department	-0.03	-0.01	0.08	-0.25	0.02	-0.04	-0.24	-0.12	0.02	-0.08
Citations (log of citations to work published 1965-1974)	0.01	-0.14	0.43	-0.03	0.00	-0.25	-0.26	-0.04	0.12	0.01
Productivity (log of papers published 1965-1974)	0.09	0.03	0.36	0.01	-0.02	-0.11	-0.27	-0.08	0.17	0.10
Years funded 1970-1974	0.13	-0.01	0.28	0.21	0.17	-0.21	-0.11	0.05	0.08	0.18
Mean rating	0.07	0.06	0.29	0.08	-0.21	0.29	0.07	0.33	0.38	0.07

proportion of requested funds. In general, the correlations suggest that, at most, only a small amount of the variance in the proportions of requested funds that are received can be explained by any one of these characteristics of principal investigators.

These tables represent first attempts to understand the influences on the amounts of money and the proportions of requested funds received among funded projects. But many questions remain unexamined here. For instance, we do not have data on the types of grants being funded—the extent to which some projects are labor-intensive and others are more dependent on equipment. Further, we do not know what types of cuts are made in budgets, what kinds of justification are made for the cuts, and the consequences for scientists of budgetary decisions. All these questions go far beyond these data, but all require further study. For the moment we can only tentatively conclude that there is no strong evidence that scientists of high rank receive strikingly disproportionate shares of NSF funds.

Another question about the distribution of NSF funds is whether some large and prestigious universities receive "disproportionate" amounts of money. Unfortunately, data we have collected cannot be used to answer this question. The unit of analysis for our research has been the investigator applicant, not the institution. Therefore, the relatively low correlations between rank of current department and amount of money received reported in Table 61 do not tell us anything about the amount of money going to particular institutions. The data on the correlation between rank of current department and proportion of funds received reported in Table 61 suggest that, if indeed some institutions are receiving a "disproportionate" amount of money, it is probably because they have more scientists applying and these scientists apply for larger grants.

MONITORING RESEARCH PERFORMANCE

Aside from the work directly involved with the decision-making process, the program directors have one other important task. They must determine how NSF resources given to investigators are being used. Thus, they must monitor the work of principal investigators. This is extremely important not only because the Foundation demands that funds be used for the purposes for which they were requested and given, but also because many principal investigators seek renewals of their grants.

The program directors monitor grant activity in a number of different ways. The most obvious strategy is evaluating the publications that come out of the funded work. As one program director put it:

On renewals, people will go through and review what they [applicants] have done on previous proposals. They will list their publications, and usually I am familiar enough with the areas to know if it is really good or significant, or if they're just publishing for the sake of it.

Although publications do provide some indication of progress, some program directors are reluctant to deny requests for renewals on the basis of low publication rates. As one said:

The only question I have is, "Is he going to stop working?" As long as there is evidence that he is working, that's O.K. Most people feel they would rather not publish, than publish crap. Most of the people to whom we give continuing grants we feel are like that.

Evaluation of work is also done by visiting research settings. Such site visits provide information about both the principal investigators and the work. This was described in the following way:

In a site visit, we make sure that the principal investigator is not sitting in a room talking to us, but that the rest of the staff is there in the room and they all have a chance to say something, and the grad students are there too. We don't want a snow job. We want to get the complete picture of what is going on.

Our intensive interviews with program directors, panel members, and other members of the NSF hierarchy suggested that there is no systematic attempt to monitor the outcomes of research grants. The scientific community is heavily relied upon to give feedback to the Foundation in the form of evaluations on subsequent grant applications. Almost nothing is done with the informal records of output that accumulate in the files of program directors. Recently, the NSF has taken steps to systematize the collection of information about research publications based on NSF-sponsored research. At the termination of grants, principal investigators must fill out forms listing all research publications produced by funded activity. To date, this information is not available to program directors for their use in evaluating the results of their prior funding decisions. Moreover, publications resulting from grants frequently come out after formal termination of the grants.

Criteria for
Selection of Grants

NOTE: The content of the following pages (through page 171) consists of facsimiles of materials used by the National Science Foundation in collecting information used as part of the data base of this report.

We have referred to the criteria that reviewers are asked to use in evaluating grant proposals. In a publication entitled, "Criteria for the Selection of Research Projects by the National Science Foundation," the NSF (1975b) lists them. They are grouped in four categories:

Category A

Criteria relating to competent performance of research—the technical adequacy of the performer and of his institutional base:

1. The scientist's training, past performance record, and estimated potential for future accomplishment.
2. The scientist's demonstrated awareness of previous and alternative approaches to his problem.
3. Probable adequacy of available or obtainable instrumentation and technical support.

Category B

Criteria relating to the internal structure of science itself:

4. Probability that the research will lead to important discoveries or valid, significant conceptual generalizations within its field of science or (in the most favorable cases) extending to other fields as well.

5. Probability that the research will lead to significant improvements or innovations of investigative method—again with possible extension to other fields of science.

Category C

Criteria relating to utility or relevance:

6. Probability that the research can serve as the basis for new invention or improved technology.

7. Probable contribution of the research to technology assessment—that is, to estimating and predicting the direct and indirect, intended and unintended effects of existing or proposed technologies.

8. Identification of an immediate programatic context and uses of the anticipated research results.

Category D

Criteria relating to future and long-term scientific potential of the United States:

9. Probable influence of the research upon the capabilities, interests, and careers of participating graduate students, postdoctoral associates, and other junior researchers.

10. Probability that the research will lead to radiation and diffusion, not only of technical results, but also of standards of workmanship and a tradition of excellence in the field.

11. Anticipated effect upon the institutional structure of U.S. science.

According to this document, the first three criteria are "vigorously applied" in all programs and the last three are always "kept in view." The document further discusses the special emphases that characterize particular programs. In the sphere of basic research, the emphasis is "overwhelmingly" on the criteria of scientific merit (4 and 5). Consideration is also given to the utility criteria (6 and 7) in a more general way and "considerable direct weight" is given to criteria 9-11. In addition, the following are said to be encouraged by the Foundation:

1. Participation in research by graduate students.
2. Open publication of research results in the standard literature.
3. Widest possible access to unique facilities for interested and competent scientists.
4. Emphasis upon originality, elegance, and economy of method in university research.

A-5

NATIONAL SCIENCE FOUNDATION

PROPOSAL RATING SHEET

Reviewer: _____   Proposal No.: _____

Investigator: _____

Institution: _____

Please return to: _____

If possible by: _____

Comments *(Continue on additional sheet if necessary)*

_____

_____

_____

_____

_____

_____

OVERALL RATING   Signature of reviewer: _____

☐ EXCELLENT   Other suggested reviewers (optional):

☐ VERY GOOD   _____

☐ GOOD   *Verbatim but anonymous copies of reviews will be sent only to the principal investigator/project direc-*

☐ FAIR   *tor on request. Subject to this NSF policy and applicable laws, including the Freedom of Information*

☐ POOR   *Act, 5 USC 552, reviewers' comments will be given maximum protection from disclosure.*

NSF Form 173, Jan. 1976

162

The staff of the National Science Foundation frequently needs to call on scientists and other specialists outside the Foundation for advice and guidance in appraising the many requests it receives. For this reason I am asking you to assist us in evaluating the scientific merit of the project described in the enclosed proposal.

The criteria for evaluation and the details of current policies and procedures are described in the enclosed instructions for reviewers. Some of the policies and procedures have changed as of January 1, 1976, so please read the instructions carefully even if you have reviewed proposals for us in the past. Please make special note of the new policy on providing verbatim copies of reviews. *We would like to add to our lists of highly qualified reviewers. Your suggestions, especially of young, women, and minority scientists would be appreciated.*

Thank you for participating in the review processes. Your assistance is vital in assuring that each proposal is evaluated fairly, critically, and promptly.

Sincerely yours,

J. CHRISTOPHER CORDARO
Program Director for Genetic Biology

Enclosures

163

INSTRUCTIONS FOR REVIEWERS OF GENETIC BIOLOGY PROPOSALS

Your critical review of the merits of the project will be of great value. Aspects that may enter into such an evaluation include the relative importance, feasibility, and conceptual framework of the project. You may also wish to consider the capacity of the investigators to conduct successfully the contemplated project, as evidenced by their description of developments in the field; their presentation of the proposed project; and their training and research contributions. If the facilities described seem inadequate, this should be noted.

Please enter your overall rating of the scientific merit of the proposal at the bottom of the rating sheet, using the following guidelines:

EXCELLENT: Highly meritorious and deserving of top priority for funding. This rating should be reserved for truly excellent proposals but should be used without hesitation when warranted.

VERY GOOD: Proposals considered superior, both for the intrinsic merit of the project and the ability or potential of the investigator, but having secondary priority.

GOOD: Quality sufficiently high to warrant consideration for support but definitely with tertiary priority.

FAIR: Unsupportable in present form; might merit consideration for support if resubmitted with major changes.

POOR: Unsupportable.

Check two adjacent boxes if your rating falls between two categories. Budgetary aspects should not enter into the rating, but comments on the budget are helpful.

Duplicate rating sheets are enclosed, together with a preaddressed envelope for the return of one of these sheets to us *by the date stamped* in the upper right-hand corner. You may keep the other sheet if you wish.

The Foundation receives proposals in confidence and is responsible for protecting the confidentiality of their contents. For this reason, we ask that you refrain from copying, quoting, or otherwise using material from this proposal. If you believe that a colleague can make a substantive contribution to the review, please consult me before disclosing either the contents of the proposal or the applicant's name. When you have completed your review or if, for some reason, you find yourself unable to respond to this request, please destroy the proposal.

Verbatim copies of reviews, ratings, and *associated correspon-*

dence will be sent to the principal investigator/project director on request. The copies will not contain your name, the name of your institution, or names that might constitute an invasion of the privacy of others. Subject to this Foundation policy and applicable laws, including the Freedom of Information Act, 5 USC 552, your participation as a reviewer and the content of your review will be given the maximum protection from disclosure.

The Foundation will publish annually a list of the names and addresses of persons who have reviewed proposals. Individuals will not, however, be identified with specific proposals. In this way the Foundation can publicly acknowledge your service as a reviewer and at the same time protect the confidentiality of your comments.

I am enclosing a proposal for your review.

The success of the Foundation's effort to strengthen scientific development through the wise use of public funds rests, fundamentally, upon the interest of individual scientists in sharing with us the responsibilities for insuring the scientific integrity of our programs. The careful and prompt evaluation of grant proposals is a vital part of this effort. Your assistance is, therefore, greatly appreciated.

Please comment as freely and with as much detail as possible. Your comparison of the merits of the enclosed proposal with others you may have reviewed in the past, and a comparison of the merits of the individual investigators with others in the field, would be of considerable value. I would also appreciate your suggestions of other possible reviewers.

The Foundation receives proposals in confidence and is responsible for protecting the confidentiality of their contents. For this reason, we ask that you refrain from copying, quoting, or otherwise using material from this proposal. If you believe that a colleague can make a substantive contribution to the review, please consult me before disclosing either the contents of the proposal or the applicant's name. When you have completed your review or if, for some reason, you find yourself unable to respond to this request, please destroy the proposal.

Verbatim copies of reviews, ratings, and associated correspondence will be sent to the principal investigator on request. The copies will not contain your name, the name of your institution, or material that might constitute an invasion of the privacy of others. Subject to this Foundation policy and applicable laws, including the Freedom of Information Act, 5 USC 552, your participation as a reviewer and the content of your review will be given the maximum protection from disclosure possible.

The Foundation will publish annually a list of the names and addresses of persons who have reviewed proposals. Individuals will not, however, be identified with specific proposals. In this way the Foundation can publicly acknowledge your service as a reviewer and at the same time protect the confidentiality of your participation.

Sincerely yours,

B. R. AGINS
Program Director for Applied Mathematics and Statistics

166

TO REVIEWERS OF MATHEMATICAL SCIENCES PROPOSALS:

Experience has shown that a somewhat discursive review, which describes the various pros and cons that have gone into making up the final judgment, is the most helpful for comparing the relative merits of proposals.

It is important that ratings shall reflect your opinion of the technical merits of the proposal and the qualifications of the investigators but shall be independent of the amount requested. However, separate recommendations concerning the proposed budget and general magnitude of the research program will be appreciated, since budgets of all proposals are adjusted before a grant is awarded.

To aid in the uniform rating of proposals, the following definitions of the rating terms are supplied.

EXCELLENT: Important research problems being undertaken by qualified mathematicians who can be expected to make substantial progress; presents an opportunity for a major contribution to basic knowledge; should be supported regardless of budgetary limitations.

VERY GOOD: Does not quite measure up to the previous category insofar as the research problem may be of somewhat lesser significance, or there may be some question concerning the ability of the investigator to carry through the complete program; should be supported.

GOOD: Worthwhile research being undertaken by competent mathematicians, but more routine in nature; may be supported if funds are available.

FAIR: Research proposal has serious deficiency that decreases probability of successful completion; not deserving of support in present form.

POOR: Inappropriate, technically unsatisfactory, or of a purely routine nature; not deserving of support.

Unless the reviewer specifically requests otherwise, certain review comments may be anonymously supplied to the proposer for his assistance and guidance.

The time and effort of reviewers is a vital part of the contribution to mathematical research made by the National Science Foundation. We thank you very much for your assistance.

Proposals submitted to the Engineering Division of the National Science Foundation are evaluated with the assistance of outside reviewers who are competent in the appropriate technical areas. Primary emphasis is placed on the technical merit of the proposal and the probable contribution of the work to the understanding of fundamental engineering principles. We are generally not concerned with specific applications or with answers to particular problems.

We would like to request your evaluation of the enclosed proposal. The proposal should be treated as a privileged document. The Foundation receives proposals in confidence and is responsible for protecting the confidentiality of their contents. For this reason, we ask that you refrain from copying, quoting, or otherwise using material from this proposal. If you believe that a colleague can make a substantive contribution to the review, please consult me before disclosing either the contents of the proposal or the applicant's name. When you have completed your review or if, for some reason, you find yourself unable to respond to this request, please return the proposal in the enclosed franked envelope.

Verbatim copies of reviews, ratings, and associated correspondence will be sent to the principal investigator/project director on request. The copies will not contain your name, the name of your institution, or names that might constitute an invasion of the privacy of others. Subject to this Foundation policy and applicable laws, including the Freedom of Information Act, 5 USC 552, your participation as a reviewer and the content of your review will be given the maximum protection from disclosure.

The Foundation will publish annually a list of the names and addresses of persons who have reviewed proposals. Individuals will not, however, be identified with specific proposals. In this way the Foundation can publicly acknowledge your service as a reviewer and at the same time protect the confidentiality of your comments.

A rating sheet, our definition of the rating terms, and a franked envelope for return of the proposal and your evaluation are enclosed. We hope that you will be able to undertake this task for us. If you are unable to complete the review or feel it is not close enough to your technical area, perhaps you can suggest names of other reviewers.

Any assistance you may be able to provide in making the evaluation will be appreciated.

Sincerely yours,

CHARLES A. BABENDREIER
Program Director, Structural Materials and Geotechnical Engineering
Engineering Division

TO REVIEWERS OF NSF ENGINEERING DIVISION
PROPOSALS:

The Engineering Division supports meritorious research that promises to advance significantly the basic engineering capabilities of the country. Such research in engineering includes the investigation of principles and techniques involved in the design of engineering systems and the analysis and synthesis of processes and systems that contribute to the mastery of the environment.

The following definitions of our standard rating terms are supplied for your guidance in evaluating the attached proposal. Reviewers are asked to interpret the definitions broadly rather than in a restricted way.

EXCELLENT: The problem is very important and well defined in the proposal. The investigators are highly competent and fully capable of doing the job. Strongly deserves support.

VERY GOOD: The problem is important and adequately defined in the proposal. The investigators are competent, and the research will contribute to their growth. Deserves support.

GOOD: The problem may be important, but the research is not well defined. The approach is routine but might contribute to graduate education or developing the potential of the principal investigator. The proposal is marginal in its present form.

FAIR: The problem is probably unimportant or not well enough defined in the proposal to allow evaluation. The approach is questionable. The proposal is not deserving of support in its present form.

POOR: The problem is unimportant, subprofessional, or has been solved by others.

Note: The Foundation will be pleased to receive comments regarding the proposed budget, but this factor should not influence your overall merit rating, since the budgets of all proposals are adjusted prior to awarding a grant.

TO: REVIEWERS OF RESEARCH PROPOSALS FOR THE NATIONAL SCIENCE FOUNDATION, DIVISION OF SOCIAL SCIENCES

CRITERIA OF JUDGMENT: Primary emphasis should be placed on the scientific merit of the project. The importance of the scientific problems addressed in the proposal, the conceptual framework of the project, the feasibility of the research strategy, and the competence of the investigator are all appropriate criteria for judgment.

BUDGET: Comments on the appropriateness of the budget for carrying out the work proposed are solicited, but budget aspects should not influence your overall merit rating. Budgets can be adjusted by the NSF staff if an award is to be made.

CONFIDENTIALITY OF PROPOSALS: Please treat the proposal as a privileged document; no material from it should be copied, quoted, or otherwise used without permission of the author, nor should the author's name be revealed in connection with this proposal. If you believe that a colleague can make a substantive contribution to the review, please consult before disclosing either the contents of the proposal or the applicant's name. When you have completed the review, or if you are unable to do it, please destroy the proposal.

CONFIDENTIALITY OF REVIEWS: To acknowledge our debt to reviewers and to inform the public, the Foundation will publish annually a list of the names and addresses of all persons who have assisted us by providing reviews. There will be no identification with specific proposals.

Verbatim copies of reviews, ratings and associated correspondence will be sent, on request, to the principal investigator/project director. These copies will be edited to remove your name and institutional identification and to avoid compromising the privacy of third parties whom you might mention but may not be retyped or otherwise changed to remove other information which might reveal your identity. Your comments and identity will, of course, be available to Foundation staff processing the proposal and to its Advisory Panels. Except for these Foundation policies, your participation as a reviewer and the content of your review will be given maximum protection from disclosure under applicable laws, including the Freedom of Information Act, 5 USC 552.

Any letter accompanying your review will be considered part of it and will be available to the investigator also, subject to the limitations mentioned above.

ENCLOSURES: Along with one copy of each proposal are three rating sheets—two copies to be returned to us in the return postage-paid envelope provided and one copy for your files. The review would be most helpful to us if the rating sheet could be returned by the date indicated. **PLEASE SIGN ONLY THE ORIGINAL. Please return original and one copy.**

B | Sample, Data, and Methods

SAMPLE

In selecting the 10 programs for study we considered the form of peer review system used. We included some programs that used only *ad hoc* mail reviews and some that used a combination of *ad hoc* mail and panel reviews. We also considered the disciplinary context of the program. We wanted to sample programs in the physical, biological, and social sciences and in engineering. The other criterion was the size of the program. We decided to include the larger rather than the smaller programs because they would include a more significant portion of all NSF activity. The 10 programs selected for analysis were: algebra, anthropology, biochemistry, chemical dynamics, ecology, economics, fluid mechanics, geophysics, meteorology, and solid-state physics. Of these, algebra, chemical dynamics, fluid mechanics, meteorology, and solid-state physics use only *ad hoc* mail review; the others use panel and mail reviews. In the geophysics section no data are kept on the ratings by panel members.

Within each program, in selecting cases for quantitative analysis we included only applications that required a new set of reviews in fiscal year 1975. We included only those applications requesting funds for new research projects. Using the basic research grant requiring a set of reviews as the unit of analysis, we chose from each program a systematic random sample of 50 grant applications that were successful and 50 that were unsuccessful. We excluded all committed renewals because the projects had been funded for more than 1 year, if funds were available. In these cases, new reviews are not obtained. We also excluded dissertation grants, travel grants, and conference grants because the criteria used in evaluating applications for these are apt to differ significantly from those used in evaluating applications for basic research.

We stratified the sample of applicants on the dependent variable, decision (i.e., 50 percent successful and 50 percent unsuccessful). We did so for two reasons. First, we wanted to make sure that the amount of variance in the dependent variable was not significantly greater in one field than in the others, since differing amounts of variance on the dependent variable could affect the size of the correlation coefficients. Second, we wanted enough acceptances and rejections to ensure statistically accurate pictures of both. Since we stratified on the dependent variable, we cannot generalize our results to all the applications in the 10 programs without using a weighting procedure because in some of the programs, our stratified random sample over-represents or under-represents successful applications. Presumably, successful and unsuccessful applications may differ in some significant ways.

Since some of the program samples over-represented or under-represented successful applicants, we wanted to make sure that this did not affect the substantive conclusions reached. In order to do this, we examined the algebra program, in which the proportion of acceptances in the sample differed by the widest margin from that in the population, repeating the entire analysis using a weighted sample that corresponded to the population. The results of this analysis were virtually identical with those reported for the algebra program throughout the report. As an example we present below the results of 20 regression equations that compare the estimated R^2 from point probit analysis for both the unweighted and weighted samples:

TABLE B-1 Proportion of Variance Explained on Ratings by Nine Independent Variables: Algebra Program

Independent Variable	Unweighted Sample	Weighted Sample
Citations to recent work	0.06	0.07
Citations to older work	0.03	0.01
Number of papers published	0.00	0.01
Rank of present department	0.07	0.05
Rank of Ph.D. department	0.04	0.03
Type of current institution (Ph.D. or not)	0.01	0.00
Professional age	0.00	0.00
Academic rank	0.03	0.03
Years funded 1970-1974	0.05	0.05
All nine variables	0.17	0.16

The probit estimates for the other tables did not differ by more than a point in the comparison of the weighted and unweighted samples. We may conclude that stratification on the dependent variable probably had no substantive influence on the probit findings reported in this report, and examination of the tabular data and ordinary regression analysis yielded the same conclusion.

The final sample in each program includes slightly more than 50 grants in each category. When we initially selected the sample and requested the jackets, some could not be located or were not available. Substitutions were made. Later, however, we obtained the missing jackets and added these to the files. A comparison of the missing jackets with the ones given to us on a first request revealed no systematic differences between the two. Thus, the final sample in each field generally contains somewhat more than 100 applications. Many of the proposals involve more than one principal investigator. For these cases we collected data on all the principal investigators.

The principal investigator, rather than the grant, is used as the unit of analysis in the quantitative analysis. Thus, if a particular grant had more than one principal investigator, each was treated as a separate unit. The analysis, then, focuses on the probability of different types of scientists receiving NSF grants. We thought that perhaps the probability of a principal investigator getting a grant would be affected by the status of his coprincipal investigator. We used two statistical comparisons to see whether our conclusions were affected by the way in which coprincipal investigators were treated. First, we compared two separate correlation matrices for the variables in the data set—one including grants with more than one principal investigator, the other omitting those grants. The correlations differed by no more than a few points. In the second comparison we identified each grant with the most eminent principal investigator, using citations to past work as the indicator of eminence. Then, with the grant as the unit of analysis, we repeated our correlation matrix and, once again, found that the correlations with the dependent variable, decision, differed by no more than a few points. Since 19 percent of the grants had more than one principal investigator, this is an expected conclusion. Using the principal investigator as the unit of analysis did not distort the results in any substantive way.

We encountered one other problem in selecting the sample. Some of the principal investigators who appeared on our list of declined applications also appeared on our list of granted applications or were current recipients on committed renewals. Inclusion of these investigators could distort the results, since the criteria in awarding a scientist a concurrent NSF grant might differ from those used in deciding whether or not he or she should be funded at all (NSF Peer Review Study, 1975a, p. 8). Therefore, we excluded from the sample all principal investigators on declined proposals who were concurrently being funded on other NSF grants in the program. When such cases turned up in our sample, we substituted the next grant on the list of rejected applications.[1]

The two tables below provide information about the level of activity in the programs we studied.

Table B-2 presents data on the actions taken by each of the 10 programs in fiscal year 1975. The first column shows the total number of actions taken by the program. This varies from a high of 419 for anthropology to a low of 140 for fluid mechanics. The second column shows the number of new research grants applied for and the last column shows the proportion of these applications that were funded. This varies from a low of 30 percent for algebra to a high of 63 percent for geophysics. This success rate may be an indicator of the amount of "proposal pressure" on each program. The extent to which such pressure influences the peer review system is not analyzed in this report. It is, however, a significant question and requires further research.

Table B-3 presents the financial statistics for each of the 10 programs for fiscal year 1975. Some of these statistics are based on estimates from our sample because the NSF did not have the data available. The first column shows the total amount of money spent by each program. The second column shows the amount of money applied for in new grant applications. The third column gives the proportion of new grant money applied for that was awarded. This proportion is a measure of the dollar pressure on the program. This varies from a low of 23 percent for chemical dynamics to a high of 56 percent for meteorology. The

---

[1]It turned out that we were not completely successful in eliminating from the list of declined applicants all scientists currently receiving NSF support. We were able to check only whether these scientists were currently receiving NSF support in the particular program we were studying. Thus, for example, we could only tell whether a scientist turned down in chemical dynamics was currently receiving money from the chemical dynamics program. We could not tell whether that scientist was receiving money from some other program. We later found that several of our declined scientists were, indeed, receiving money from some other NSF programs. This applies to only a small number of the 1,200 scientists in the sample. We also were not able to determine whether principal investigators on declined projects were concurrently receiving funds from other government or nongovernment agencies. In some fields, such as biochemistry, there is a stronger possibility of this than in others, such as mathematics. Further, we do not know how often projects are declined explicitly because of alternative sources of support. Review of the proposal jackets suggests that this number is probably quite small.

TABLE B-2 Proposal Activity for 10 Programs, FY 1975

Program	(1) Total	(2) New Grants Awarded	(3) Continuing Grants	(4) Dissertation/Travel/ Conference Grants	(5) Declinations		(6) Proportion of New Grants Funded (Excluding Dissertation Travel/Conference Grants), %
					Grants	Dissertation/ Conference	
Algebra	308	61	104	0	143	0	30
Anthropology	419	77	44	88	111	99	41
Biochemistry	378	122	120	10	125	1	49
Chemical Dynamics	236	51	92	1	91	1	36
Ecology	285	82	42	22	106	33	44
Economics	269	75	55	10	121	8	38
Fluid Mechanics	140	59	22	4	54	1	52
Geophysics	185	91	40	0	54	0	63
Meteorology	186	81	43	8	54	0	60
Solid-State Physics	293	71	114	6	101	1	41

TABLE B-3 Financial Statistics for 10 Programs, FY 1975

Program	(1) Total Funds Awarded[a] (New and Continuing)	(2) Total New Grant Funds Applied for[b]	(3) Proportion of New Funds Granted Out of Total Funds Applied for	(4) Proportion of Total Funds Committed	(5) Mean Value of New Award[c]	(6) Proportion of New Funds Granted to Awardees
Algebra	1,963,005	2,547,653	0.28	0.63	11,897	0.73
Anthropology[d]	3,041,698	6,267,613	0.31	0.36	25,138	0.81
Biochemistry	6,865,056	10,812,705	0.32	0.50	28,368	0.59
Chemical Dynamics	4,590,300	7,060,231	0.23	0.64	32,100	0.74
Ecology	3,143,400	5,912,246	0.35	0.34	25,350	0.76
Economics	4,389,970	8,831,890	0.29	0.42	33,769	0.75
Fluid Mechanics	2,099,439	3,363,205	0.45	0.27	25,919	0.85
Geophysics	3,584,946	5,001,117	0.50	0.31	27,366	0.74
Meteorology	4,766,436	5,553,036	0.56	0.35	38,439	0.82
Solid-State Physics	5,752,945	6,048,056	0.37	0.61	31,097	0.79

[a]The data on proposal activity are drawn from "Program Officers Workload Status Report Fiscal Year 1975 Proposals and Actions" (an NSF document). Although this report contains funding information, certain limitations prohibit us from using this information. First, it only provides the amount received by grant recipients and the amount applied for by declined applicants, and second, there is no specification of the time period for successful grants, unsuccessful requests, and continuing awards, making it impossible to determine how funds are distributed on a yearly basis.

Because of these limitations, all figures presented in this table are estimates based on our sample. Total new awards was computed by multiplying the mean award for the sample (for each program) by the total number of new awards given by the program. Total continuing awards was computed by multiplying the mean award for the sample by the total number of continuing awards. (We used the new-award mean, since we cannot determine the value of continuing awards from NSF data.)

[b]This figure is the sum of the mean value of requests by successful and unsuccessful applicants in the sample multiplied by the actual number of applicants in each category.

[c]This figure is a result of dividing the estimated total amount of new funds granted by the number of recipients of new grants.

[d]Dissertation grants and requests are not included in these figures. In this field, $431,800 was distributed for dissertation support. This represents 12 percent of the program's total budget. Forty-four percent of requests for the support were granted.

Two other programs, ecology and economics, also provide dissertation support, but the amounts involved are quite small (less than 2 percent of total budget). Conference and travel funds are also granted by other programs but this activity is quite minimal.

177

influence of such dollar pressure on the operation of peer review requires further research.

The fourth column of Table B-3 shows the proportion of program budget spent on committed renewals. This tells us the extent to which the various programs commit money to relatively long-term projects. The reasons for such decisions and the consequences should be further analyzed.

The fifth column shows the mean dollar amount for new awards, and the last column shows for grant recipients the amount of money awarded divided by the amount applied for. This various from a low of 59 percent to a high of 82 percent. Most of these percentages are around 75 percent, indicating that the average grant recipient gets about three-fourths of what he applies for. The low figure for biochemistry deserves further research. It may be that in this program an effort is being made to "spread the money around." The reasons for this decision and the consequences should be analyzed.

DATA

After selecting the sample we collected data on the principal investigators. The data sources included: the grant jacket, which contained the peer review material, a curriculum vitae of the principal investigator, and a list of his publications; *American Men and Women of Science* (AMWS); the rankings of graduate departments published by the American Council on Education (ACE); and the *Science Citation Index* (SCI). The data contained information on the status of the principal investigators in the sciences; indicators of their scientific track record; peer review ratings; and decisions. The variables constructed from these data are:

- Chronological age of principal investigator.
- Professional age of principal investigator (number of years since acquiring Ph.D.). In this report we have divided the applicants into those who obtained their Ph.D. prior to 1970 and those who obtained it in 1970 or after.
- Prestige ranking of Ph.D. department (obtained from the 1964 ACE rankings). Depending upon how many departments were included in the ACE survey, we divided them into four or five groups. In those parts of the analysis in which we could not use pair deletion, we assigned a low score to all cases for which the applicant's department was not

included in the ACE survey or for which the applicant worked in a nonacademic setting. We did this because, *on the average*, unranked departments and nonacademic institutions have lower prestige than ranked departments. For those parts of the analysis in which we were able to delete cases with missing data, we compared the results using deletion with those using a low score for missing data. In all cases the results were substantively similar.

Measuring ranks of academic departments was relatively difficult in geophysics and meteorology. The subject closest to geophysics included in the ACE survey was geology, and meteorology was not included at all. For those two fields we sent questionnaires to members of the National Academy of Sciences and asked them to rate all the departments for which we needed information. We received usable responses from 15 geophysicists and 9 meteorologists. For these two programs, rank of Ph.D. department was obtained from scores computed from these questionnaires.

• Type of present institution (this was coded dichotomously as a Ph.D.-granting institution or all other institutions).[2]

• Rank of current academic department (for those teaching in Ph.D.-granting institutions we used the 1969 ACE rankings). This variable was coded the same as rank of Ph.D. department. For those parts of the analysis in which we could not use pair deletion, we assigned all missing cases, scientists in unranked institutions, and scientists in nonacademic institutions the lowest possible score. This is based upon the assumption that most of these scientists were employed at institutions with lower prestige than ACE-ranked graduate departments. Scores of geophysicists and meteorologists were determined from the questionnaires returned by NAS members.

• Academic rank (coded as follows: 1 = researcher; 2 = postdoctoral; 3 = instructor, lecturer; 4 = assistant professor; 5 = associate professor; 6 = full professor).

• Amount of money applied for in first year of grant.

• Number of single-authored papers published between 1965 and

[2]At first we coded the principal investigators as coming from Ph.D.-granting institutions, other academic institutions, government agencies, private industry, foundation or other private research institutes, and other institutions. It turned out that there were so few scientists in each of the categories other than Ph.D.-granting institutions that the basic distinction was simply whether or not the scientist worked at a Ph.D.-granting or some other institution. Therefore, we decided to dichotomize this variable.

1974 (obtained from the source index of the *Science Citation Index*, 1965-1974).[3]

• Number of first-authored papers published between 1965 and 1974 (obtained from the source index, SCI).

• Number of second-authored papers published between 1965 and 1974 (obtained from the source index, SCI).

• Total number of papers published between 1965 and 1974 (the sum of variables 9-11). For the analysis we used a log transformation to the base 10. For anthropology and economics we used a log transformation of the productivity index.

• Number of citations in 1974 to work published between 1970 and 1974 (obtained from 1974 SCI).[4]

• Citations in 1974 to work published between 1965 and 1969 (obtained from 1974 SCI).

• Number of citations in 1974 to papers on which the author was not first author published between 1965 and 1974 (obtained from 1974 SCI).

• Total number of citations to work published between 1965 and 1974 (the sum of variables 13-15). We used a log transformation to the base 10. Citation data for anthropology and economics do not include citations to papers on which the author was not first author.

• Citations in 1974 to work published prior to 1965 (obtained from 1974 SCI). We used a log transformation to the base 10.

• Number of years between 1970 and 1974 in which the principal investigator has received funds from the NSF.

• Rating given the application by the program director.

• Ratings given the application by each mail reviewer and by each panel member, where such data were recorded.

• Type of institution at which each reviewer was located.

• Prestige of the reviewer's department for those reviewers at Ph.D.-granting institutions.

• Geographical locations of reviewer and applicant.

• Decision: accept = 2, decline = 1.

Data were set up on two different files for each program. On one file the applicant was the unit of analysis; on the other the unit of analysis

[3]For anthropology and economics the publication data were obtained not from the source index of the *Social Science Citation Index*, since this goes back only to 1972, but from curricula vitae contained in the grant jacket. For these two fields we used a productivity index. We classified publications into one of the following weighted categories: books weighted 10; edited books weighted 4; profesional articles weighted 2; chapters in books weighted 2; applied articles and reports weighted 1.

[4]Citations for anthropologists and economists were obtained from the 1974 volume of the *Social Science Citation Index*.

was the pair of applicant and mail reviewer. The latter file was used in sections 2 and 3 and the former in section 5.

METHODS[5]

We have used probit regression analysis to deal with the problem raised by using the dichotomous variable, decision, as our dependent variable.

Theoretically, and in an ideal world, all proposals could be ordered unambiguously from best to worst, and that ordering is what we would like to be able to predict. But in the real world, even if that ordering were possible, it would be in some sense irrelevant, for at some point on the continuum, a break must be made between proposals to be funded and those to be refused. Indeed, it is this funded-refused dichotomy (decision) that we have frequently used as our dependent variable.

Clearly, however, we must conceive of the funded proposals as ranging from excellent to barely fundable and the refused proposals as ranging down from practically fundable to clearly rejectable. This distinction between an unobserved continuum of possible ratings and the observed dichotomous variable (decision) was formally incorporated in the probit regression models that were fit to the data in this study, as discussed below.

In order to specify the probit model, first introduce $Y_1, Y_2, \cdots, Y_n$ as independent random variables that can assume arbitrary real values. The random variable Y_j is an unobservable rating for the purpose of the program director's decision making. It is not the same as the reviewers' ratings but is the variable in the program director's mind, summarizing the information he has about j in terms of a numerical index that determines whether the grant is above or below the critical cutoff value that is called μ_1 below. Next let $Z_1, Z_2, \cdots, Z_n$ be the observed decisions defined by the rule

$$Z_j = \begin{cases} 0 \text{ if } j\text{th proposal is refused} \\ 1 \text{ if } j\text{th proposal is funded} \end{cases}$$

$Z_1, Z_2, \cdots, Z_n$ are defined in terms of $Y_1, Y_2, \cdots, Y_n$ according to

[5]Professor Burton Singer, Department of Mathematical Statistics, Columbia University, and Professor Judith Tanur, Department of Sociology, State University of New York, Stony Brook, worked on this description of probit analysis. Professor Singer produced the mathematical description of the probit statistics used in this report.

$$Z_j = \begin{cases} 0 & \text{if } Y_j < \mu_1 \\ 1 & \text{if } Y_j \geq \mu_1 \end{cases}$$

where μ_1 is an unobserved cutoff level at which a proposal is either funded or refused. (We can set $\mu_1 = 0$ without loss of generality in the present study.)

Now introduce the linear regression model

$$Y_j = \sum_{i=0}^{k} \beta_i X_{ij} + u_j$$

where $X_{0j} \equiv 1$; X_{ij} = value of ith independent variable for jth proposal (principal investigator). For the jth individual, the X_{ij} represent the values of different variables such as reviewer rating, citation index, rank of university. The $u_1, u_2, \cdots, u_n$ are independent, normally distributed random variables with $E(u_j) = 0$, Var $(u_j) = 1$, $1 \leq j \leq n$; and $\beta_0, \beta_1, \cdots, \beta_k$ are coefficients to be estimated. In terms of this specification we can write the probability of being refused or funded as

Prob (jth proposal is refused) = Prob $(Z_j = 0) = \Phi\left(-\sum_{i=0}^{k} \beta_i X_{ij}\right)$ (1)

where

$$\Phi(x) = \int_{-\infty}^{x} \frac{e^{-w^2/2}}{\sqrt{2\pi}} \, dw$$

and

Prob (jth proposal is funded) = Prob $(Z_j = 1) = 1 - \Phi\left(-\sum_{i=0}^{k} \beta_i X_{ij}\right)$

The nature of the linearity assumption (Eq. (1)) and the normality assumption for the error terms u_j as well as the question of whether it holds strictly (sometimes, even approximately), and our reasons for using the probit model, are discussed in section 5, page 110.

The coefficients $\beta_0, \cdots, \beta_k$ were estimated by maximum likelihood—maximizing the likelihood function

$L(Z_1, \cdots, Z_n | \beta_0, \cdots, \beta_k)$

$$= \prod_{j=1}^{n} \left[\Phi\left(-\sum_{i=0}^{k} \beta_i X_{ij}\right)\right]^{1-Z_j} \left[1 - \Phi\left(-\sum_{i=0}^{k} \beta_i X_{ij}\right)\right]^{Z_j}$$

using the computer program NPROBIT of McKelvey and Zavoina (1975).

The fit of the model (Eq. (1)) to the data was assessed by calculating the statistic $\hat{R}^2$ defined below. This measure of goodness of fit was motivated by the following considerations (see McKelvey and Zavoina, 1975, for further details):

Given the estimated coefficients $\hat{\beta}_0, \cdots, \hat{\beta}_k$, define the fitted (i.e., estimated value of) unobserved values $\hat{Y}_j$ according to

$$\hat{Y}_j = \sum_{i=0}^{k} \hat{\beta}_i X_{ij}$$

and introduce the residuals

$$e_j = Y_j - \hat{Y}_j$$

By analogy with ordinary linear regression analysis, we define the total sum of squares to be

$$S_{\text{total}}^2 = \sum_{j=1}^{n} (Y_j - \overline{Y})^2, \text{ where } \overline{Y} = n^{-1} \sum_{j=1}^{n} Y_j$$

Then writing

$$(Y_j - \overline{Y})^2 = \left[(Y_j - \hat{Y}_j) + (\hat{Y}_j - \overline{Y})\right]^2$$

and replacing $\overline{Y}$ by its approximation,

$$\hat{\overline{Y}} = \frac{1}{n} \sum_{j=1}^{n} \hat{Y}_j,$$

we introduce the plausible (for large sample size, n) approximation to S_{total}^2,

$$\hat{S}_{\text{total}}^2 = \hat{S}_{\text{explained}}^2 + \hat{S}_{\text{residual}}^2 \tag{2}$$

where

$$\hat{S}_{\text{explained}}^2 = \sum_{j=1}^{n} (\hat{Y}_j - \hat{\overline{Y}}_j)^2$$

and

$$\hat{S}_{\text{residual}}^2 = \sum_{j=1}^{n} (Y_j - \hat{Y}_j)^2$$

(The formula corresponding to Eq. (2) in ordinary linear regression is exactly satisfied without the carets, and it suggests the present approximation. In the probit model, Eq. (2) without carets is *not* satisfied exactly.) Finally, we define

$$\hat{R}^2 = \frac{\hat{S}^2_{\text{explained}}}{\hat{S}^2_{\text{total}}}$$

Since

$$\frac{1}{n} \sum_{j=1}^{n} (Y_j - \hat{Y}_j)^2 \xrightarrow[n \to \infty]{} 1 \text{ in probability}$$

under the model (1), for large n we may approximate $\hat{R}^2$ as

$$\hat{\hat{R}}^2 = \frac{\hat{S}^2_{\text{explained}}}{\hat{S}^2_{\text{explained}} + n}$$

This $\hat{\hat{R}}^2$ was utilized in the calculations of the present study, and for simplicity is referred to in section 5 simply as the probit R^2. It gives an estimate of its population counterpart, a measure of the proportion of the variance of the Y_j about $\overline{Y}$ that is explained by the X_{ij} in terms of the probit model.

As McKelvey and Zavoina (1975, p. 112) point out, the partitioning of the sum of squares (Eq. (2)) is not really legitimate for finite n. However, it is a plausible conjecture that

$$S^2_{\text{total}} \sim \hat{S}^2_{\text{total}}, \, n \to \infty$$

although a rigorous proof is not currently in hand. McKelvey and Zavoina also mention a number of possible limitations of this approach including the likelihood of overestimation by $\hat{R}^2$ of its population counterpart. Nevertheless $\hat{R}^2$, as defined above, has proved a plausible and useful quantity in other social science applications and yields conclusions in the present study that are compatible with the tabular analyses.

The probit regression program we used did not allow for paired deletion of cases with missing data. Therefore, on all variables except rank of doctoral department and rank of current department, we used the variable mean for cases with missing data. For the two rank-of-department variables we assigned all cases with "missing" data a low score.

Decision is, of course, a dichotomous dependent variable. And it was specifically for use with this dependent variable that probit was chosen. Nonetheless, it is possible to compare what the results would have been had we used regular regression analysis with those obtained from the probit analysis. A comparison is presented in Table B-4. The first two columns show the proportion of variance in decision explained by the nine characteristics of the applicants in each of the 10 programs, using both probit techniques and ordinary linear regression techniques.

As can be clearly seen from these statistics, the probit estimates are consistently higher than are the regression estimates. McKelvey and Zavoina have pointed out that the probit estimates may be too large. However, we would also expect the probit R^2 to be larger than the R^2 for regression analysis with a dichotomous dependent variable (some value less than 1), provided the normality assumption is better than the assumption that Φ can be replaced by a linear function over the domain of values of

$$\sum_i \beta_i X_{ij}$$

Although the size of the R^2 estimated by probit procedures and the proportion of variance explained by regression procedures differ, the relative magnitude of the results in the 10 different programs is approximately the same. For example, when probit is used, we find the

TABLE B-4 Variance on Funding Decision Explained by Characteristics of Principal Investigators and Ratings of Reviewers—Comparison of Probit Analysis and Regression Analysis

	R^2 Individual Variables		R^2 Mean Rating of Reviewers (and Panels Where They End)		R^2 All Variables	
Program	Probit	Regression	Probit	Regression	Probit	Regression
Algebra	0.34	0.24	0.76	0.48	0.84	0.53
Anthropology	0.17	0.11	0.83	0.55	0.86	0.59
Biochemistry	0.51	0.33	0.86	0.57	0.86	0.62
Chemical Dynamics	0.39	0.24	0.92	0.54	0.96	0.60
Ecology	0.40	0.28	0.77	0.40	0.86	0.48
Economics	0.39	0.27	0.78	0.53	0.83	0.60
Fluid Mechanics	0.37	0.20	0.58	0.38	0.71	0.45
Geophysics	0.36	0.23	0.49	0.30	0.70	0.44
Meteorology	0.24	0.17	0.92	0.55	0.94	0.57
Solid-State Physics	0.70	0.48	0.70	0.47	0.91	0.61

smallest proportion of variance explained by the nine individual variables in the program of anthropology and the largest proportion explained in solid-state physics. Exactly the same results are obtained when we use regular regression analysis. In the second column of Table B-4 we compare the estimated proportion of variance explained by the ratings of reviewers (and panel members where panels were used), using probit techniques and using regression techniques. Once again we find that the probit estimates are considerably higher than the regression estimates. In fact, the higher the correlation is in regression analysis, the greater the difference seems to be between the results from the regression analysis and those from the probit analysis. Substantively, the important part of Table B-4 is the last column, which shows how much additional variance is explained by the nine characteristics of the applicants when we add them to an equation containing the mean rating of the proposal. In algebra, for example, all nine variables and the mean rating explain 84 percent of the variance, using probit, where the mean rating alone explains 76 percent, using probit. Thus, the nine applicant characteristics increase the amount of variance explained by 8 points. Using regular regression techniques, we find that the increase in the amount of variance explained when the nine individual variables are added into the regression equation is 5 points. In general, whether we use the probit analysis or the regression analysis, the nine applicant characteristics add relatively little variance to the explained variance after mean ratings are entered into the equation.

Thus, we may conclude that both analytic techniques would lead to a similar conclusion, that is, that under the linearity assumption (Eq. (1)), mean reviewer rating of all the variables for which measurements are available is the most significant single determinant of whether or not a grant is made and that among the variables for which we have measurements, the nine characteristics of applicants do not add substantially to the predictability of whether or not a grant will be made.

The probit procedure we used is also useful for analyzing variables with a restricted range, such as reviewer ratings. (It was unnecessary to perform a separate Tobit analysis on the data.) Although conceptually the proposals could be ranked from "most meritorious" to "least meritorious," in fact the great majority of funded proposals are rated as "excellent" (1), "very good" (2), or "good" (3). This means that there is a problem of making the dependent variable discrete.

Our probit treatment of ratings of proposals was analogous to that for decisions. In particular we assume a continuum of unobserved possible ratings Y and cutoff points $\mu_1 < \mu_2 < \mu_3 < \mu_4$ such that a proposal is rated in the following response categories[6]:

$1 =$ excellent if $Y \le \mu_1$
$2 =$ very good if $\mu_1 < Y \le \mu_2$
$3 =$ good if $\mu_2 < Y \le \mu_3$
$4 =$ fair if $\mu_3 < Y \le \mu_4$
$5 =$ poor if $Y > \mu_4$

For the discussion that follows define $\mu_0 = -\infty$, $\mu_1 = 0$, $\mu_5 = +\infty$, and then let $Y_1, Y_2, \cdots, Y_n$ be independent ratings represented by the linear regression model

$$Y_j = \sum_{i=0}^{K} \beta_i X_{ij} + u_j \qquad 1 \le j \le n \qquad (3)$$

where $u_1, \cdots, u_n$ satisfy the same hypotheses as in the model of equation (1). Then represent the observed ratings by the dummy variables.

$$Z_{jk} = \begin{cases} 1 \text{ if } j\text{th rating is in the } k\text{th response category} \\ 0 \text{ otherwise} \end{cases}$$

$$= \begin{cases} 1 \text{ if } \mu_{k-1} < Y_j \le \mu_k \\ 0 \text{ otherwise} \end{cases}$$

Then the probability of the jth rating being in the kth response category is given by

$$\text{Prob } (Z_{jk} = 1) = \Phi\left(\mu_k - \sum_{i=0}^{K} \beta_i X_{ij}\right) - \Phi\left(\mu_{k-1} - \sum_{i=0}^{K} \beta_i X_{ij}\right)$$

where, again,

$$\Phi(x) = \int_{-\infty}^{x} \frac{e^{-w^2/2}}{\sqrt{2\pi}}\, dw$$

[6]The above numbering of response categories is for indexing purposes only; it is *not* to be viewed as an assignment of numerical scores.

TABLE B-5 Comparison of Results Using Probit and Regression Analysis: Dependent Variable = Rating[a]

Program	Citations to Recent Work		Rank of Current Department		NSF Funding History		All Nine Independent Variables	
	Probit R^2	Regression R^2	Probit R^2	Regression R^2	Probit R^2	Regression R^2	Probit R^2	Regression R^2
Algebra	0.09	0.06	0.07	0.07	0.06	0.05	0.19	0.17
Anthropology	0.01	0.00	0.00	—	0.00	—	0.05	0.04
Biochemistry	0.19	0.16	0.09	0.07	0.07	0.06	0.25	0.20
Chemical Dynamics	0.15	0.14	0.03	0.02	0.06	0.05	0.18	0.16
Ecology	0.01	0.01	0.02	0.02	0.02	0.02	0.05	0.06
Economics	0.10	0.08	0.14	0.13	0.09	0.08	0.23	0.21
Fluid Mechanics	0.03	0.03	0.12	0.10	0.01	0.01	0.20	0.17
Geophysics	0.08	0.07	0.03	0.03	0.01	0.01	0.10	0.09
Meteorology	0.09	0.08	0.06	0.05	0.02	0.02	0.15	0.14
Solid-State Physics	0.08	0.08	0.09	0.08	0.07	0.06	0.19	0.17

[a]Relationship is negative.

The cutoff points μ_2, μ_3, μ_4, and the regression coefficients β_0, β_1, $\cdots$, β_k were estimated using NPROBIT (see McKelvey and Zavoina, 1975) to maximize the likelihood function

$$L\left(\{Z_{jk}\}|\beta_0, \cdots, \beta_K, \mu_2, \mu_3, \mu_4\right)$$

$$= \prod_{j=1}^{n} \prod_{k=1}^{5} \left[\Phi\left(\mu_k - \sum_{i=0}^{K} \beta_i X_{ij}\right) - \Phi\left(\mu_{k-1} - \sum_{i=0}^{K} \beta_i X_{ij}\right) \right]^{Z_{jk}}$$

With the estimates β_0, β_1, $\cdots$, β_K at hand, the goodness of fit of the regression model is assessed by the same procedure as described for the case when decision was the dependent variable. The increased complexity of this case, compared with the earlier one involving only one response, means that the limitations of the $\hat{R}^2$ estimates are probably now greater.

In Table B-5 we compare the results of a probit analysis with those of a regression analysis when the dependent variable was rating. Table B-5 shows the proportion of variance explained by citations to recent work, by rank of current department, by the NSF funding history of the applicant, and by the nine variables we have used to characterize applicants. The table presents the results of a total of 40 ordinary least-squares regressions and 40 probit regression equations. As can be seen by this comparison, there is no great systematic difference between the results of the two procedures. In all cases the probit results are either exactly the same as the regression results or slightly higher. (See earlier comments about this.) Comparison of the amount of variance explained by the sum of the nine variables produces remarkably similar results. For example, in algebra the probit analysis explained 19 percent of the variance on ratings using the nine variables characterizing applicants, and the regression analysis explained 17 percent of the variance on ratings. Because the two methods yielded essentially identical results and the same substantive conclusions, we have used the regression technique, which is simpler and more widely understood. (For discussion of probit analysis and its uses, see page 110, section 5.)

Bibliography
and
References

Allison, P. D., and J. A. Stewart. 1974. "Productivity Differences Among Scientists: Evidence for Accumulative Advantage." *American Sociological Review* 39(4):596-607.

American Men and Women of Science (12th ed.). 1973. New York: Jacques Cattell Press.

Biomedical Science and Its Administration. 1965. A Study of The National Institutes of Health. Supt. of Documents, U.S. Government Printing Office, Washington, D.C.

Cain, G. G., and H. W. Watts. 1970. "Problems of Making Policy Inferences from the Coleman Report." *American Sociological Review* 35:222-42.

Carter, G. 1974. *Peer Review, Citations and Biomedical Research Policy: NIH Grants to Medical School Faculty.* Santa Monica, Calif.: Rand Corporation Report 1583-HEW.

Cartter, A. M. 1966. *An Assessment of Quality of Graduate Education.* Washington, D.C.: American Council on Education.

Cole, J., and S. Cole. 1972. "The Ortega Hypothesis." *Science* 178(4059):368-74.

Cole, J., and S. Cole. 1973. *Social Stratification in Science.* Chicago: University of Chicago Press.

Cole, S. 1977. "Scientific Reward Systems: A Comparative Analysis." Forthcoming in Robert Alun Jones, ed., *Research in Sociology of Knowledge, Sciences, and Art.* Vol. I. Greenwich, Conn.: Jai Press.

Cole, S., and H. A. Zuckerman. 1976. "The Use of ACE Ratings in Research on Science and Higher Education." Prepared for planning conference on assessment of the quality of graduate education programs in the United States, September 27-29, Woods Hole, Massachusetts.

Cole, S., J. Cole, and L. Dietrich. 1976. "Measuring Consensus in Scientific Research Areas." In Yehuda Elkana *et al.*, eds., *Science Indicators.* New York: Wiley Interscience.

Committee on Government Research of the House of Representatives. 1964. *Report.* Washington, D.C.: U.S. Government Printing Office.

Committee on Science and Technology of the U.S. House of Representatives. 1976. *National Science Foundation Peer Review*. Washington, D.C.: U.S. Government Printing Office.

Douglas, C. D., and J. C. James. 1973. "Support of New Principal Investigators by NIH: 1966 to 1972." *Science* 181:241-44.

Finney, D. J. 1952. *Probit Analysis* (2nd ed.). Cambridge, England: Cambridge University Press.

Goode, W. J. 1967. "The Protection of the Inept." *American Sociological Review* 32:5-19.

Greenberg, D. 1967. *The Politics of Pure Science*. New York: New American Library.

Groeneveld, L., N. Koller, and N. C. Mullins. 1975. "The Advisers of the United States National Science Foundation." *Social Studies of Science* 5:343-54.

Gustafson, T. 1975. "The Controversy over Peer Review." *Science* 190(4219):1060-66.

Institute for Scientific Information. 1974. *Science Citation Index*. Philadelphia.

Kuhn, T. 1962. *The Structure of Scientific Revolutions*. Chicago: University of Chicago Press.

Laveck, C. C., *et al.* 1974. "Recipients of Research Grants for NICHD: Do Age, Sex, Type of Degree Affect Funding Chances?" *Pediatrics* 53(5):706-11.

Leege, D. C. 1975. "Is Political Science Alive and Well and Living at NSF: Reflections of a Program Director at Midstream." Paper delivered at annual meeting of American Political Science Association, San Francisco, California.

Liebert, R. J. 1976. "Productivity, Favor, and Grants among Scholars," *American Journal of Sociology* 82(3):664-73.

McKelvey, R., and W. Zavoina. 1975. "A Statistical Model for the Analysis of Ordinal Level Dependent Variables." *Journal of Mathematical Sociology*, 4:103-20.

Merton, R. K. 1942. "Science and Technology in a Democratic Order." *Journal of Legal and Political Science* 1:115-26.

Merton, R. K. 1957. *Social Theory and Social Structure*. New York: The Free Press.

Merton, R. K. 1968. "The Matthew Effect in Science: The Reward and Communication Systems of Science." *Science* 199:55-63.

Morrison, D. E., and R. E. Henkel, eds. 1970. *The Significance Test Controversy*. Chicago: Aldine.

National Science Foundation. 1975a. "Peer Review and Proposal Evaluation, Staff Study." *NSF Peer Review Study*. Washington, D.C.: NSF Administration Directorate.

National Science Foundation. 1975b. *Criteria for the Selection of Research Projects by the National Science Foundation* (NSB-74-300, February 1975).

National Science Foundation. 1975c. *An Analysis of the Geographical Distribution of NSF Awards as Compared with other Selected Indicators*. Washington, D.C.: NSF Administration Directorate.

National Science Foundation. 1975d. *NSF Management Statistics*. Washington, D.C.: NSF Administration Directorate.

Office of Management and Budget. 1973. "The National Institutes of Health and National Institute of Mental Health Peer Review System." OMB Issue Paper. Unpublished.

Pfeffer, J., G. R. Salancek, and H. Leblebici. 1976. "The Effect of Uncertainty on the Use of Social Influence in Organization Decision Making." *Administrative Science Quarterly* 21:227-45.

Price, D. 1963. *Little Science, Big Science*. New York: Columbia University Press.

Roose, K. D., and C. J. Andersen. 1971. *A Rating of Graduate Programs*. Washington, D.C.: American Council on Education.

Small, H. G. 1974a. *Characteristics of Frequently Cited Papers in Chemistry*. Philadelphia: Institute for Scientific Information.

Small, H. G. 1974b. *Report on Citation Counts for National Science Foundation Grant Recipients and Non-Recipients*. Philadelphia: Institute for Scientific Information.

Useem, M. 1976. "State Production of Social Knowledge: Patterns in Government Financing of Academic Social Research." *American Sociological Review* 41(4):613-29.

U.S. Office of Science and Technology. 1965. *Biomedical Science and its Administration: A Study of the National Institutes of Health*. Washington, D.C.: U.S. Government Printing Office.

Vivona, D., and D. DoVan Quy. 1973. "Comparability of the American Cancer Society and the National Institutes of Health Peer Review System." *Cancer Research* 33(4):919.

Wilson, M. K. 1975. "The Top Twenty and the Rest: Big Chemistry and Little Funding." *Annual Review of Physical Chemistry* 26:1-16.

Wirt, J. G., A. J. Lieberman, and R. E. Levien. 1974. *R & D Management: Methods Used by Federal Agencies*. Santa Monica, Calif.: Rand Corporation Report R-1156-HEW.

Zuckerman, H. 1977. *The Scientific Elite*. New York: Free Press.

Zuckerman, H., and J. Cole. 1975. "Women in American Science." *Minerva* XIII(1)82-102.